CW00421961

Batsford's Walking Guides: The Cotswolds

Batsford's Walking Guides: The Cotswolds

*Written and compiled
by Jilly MacLeod*

BATSFORD

First published in the United Kingdom in 2011 by
Batsford
10 Southcombe Street
London
W14 0RA
An imprint of Anova Books Company Ltd

Materials kindly provided by individual organizations,
as credited at the end of each walk.

Walks on pages 28, 64 and 76 © Natural England 2011.
Material is reproduced with the permission of Natural
England, http://www.naturalengland.org.uk/copyright

ISBN 9781906388850

A CIP catalogue for this book is available from
the British Library.

20 19 18 17 16 15 14 13 12 11
10 9 8 7 6 5 4 3 2 1

Reproduction by Rival Colour Ltd, UK
Printed by 1010 Printing International Ltd, China

This book can be ordered direct from the publisher
at the website www.anovabooks.com, or try your
local bookshop.

Neither the publisher nor the author can accept
responsibility for any changes, errors or omissions
in this guide, or for any loss or injury incurred
during any of the walks.

Contents

Map of The Cotswolds

Evesham

Broadway

17

19

HEREFORD
AND
WORCESTER

Tewkesbury

Toddington

Bishop's
Cleeve

Winchcombe

5

8

Ross-
on-Wye

Cheltenham

Gloucester

Charlton
Kings

Brockworth

Cranham **14**

G L O U C E S T E R S H I R E

Painswick

4

•Monmouth

Stroud

15 **11**

Cirencester

20

Dursley **18** Nailsworth

Chepstow

7

Wotton-under-Edge

Tetbury

SOUTH

Leighterton

10

•Thornbury

13

Malmesbury

Wootton Bassett

Chipping
Sodbury

M4

GLOUCESTERSHIRE

Lyneham

CITY OF
BRISTOL

Chippenham

Bristol

Corsham

Calne

Keynsham

W I L T S H I R E

Bath

6

Melksham

Devizes

BATH AND NORTH

Bradford-on-Avon

EAST SOMERSET

WARWICKSHIRE

Ilmington

12

Shipston
on Stour

pping
npden

Banbury

NORTHAMPTON-
SHIRE

Brackley

Bloxham

Buckingham

Moreton-
in-Marsh

Deddington

Stow-on-
the-Wold

3 Chipping Norton

6

ourton-on-
ne-Water

2 Charlbury

M40

BUCKINGHAM-
SHIRE

Bicester

Milton under
Wychwood **1**

Woodstock

Kidlington

Burford

9

Thame

Witney

Oxford

OXFORDSHIRE

Kingston Bagpuize

chlade

Faringdon

Highworth

JDON

windon

KEY TO MAP

1) Five Fields Walk
2) Cornbury Park Walk
3) Oxfordshire Ramble
4) 'Cider with Rosie' Walk
5) Cleeve Hill Common Ring
6) Bath Skyline Walk
7) Wotton to Waterloo
8) Historic Winchcombe Walk
9) Windrush Valley Walk
10) In the Footsteps of a King
11) Golden Valley Walk

12) North Face of the Cotswolds
13) Ancient Woodland Walk
14) Cranham, Cooper's and
    the Beechwoods
15) Cotswold Canal Walk
16) Mills and Meadows Walk
17) Broadway Tower Walk
18) String of Pearls Walk
19) Three Cotswold Villages
20) Woodchester Park
    Boathouse Trail

Introduction

With its picturesque villages, rolling hills, ancient woodlands and tranquil valleys, the Cotswolds is known as one of the most beautiful areas in Britain, comprising a quintessentially English landscape. It is also designated an Area of Outstanding Natural Beauty (AONB), the largest of 40 such areas in England and Wales, where the precious landscape and rich biodiversity is safeguarded in the interests of the nation. The term 'Cotswold' refers specifically to an area of gently rolling hills in south-west England, roughly bounded on three sides by motorways – the M4, M5 and M40 – and stretching 160km (100 miles) from Bath in the south to Chipping Norton and beyond in the north, covering much of Gloucestershire and parts of Worcestershire, Warwickshire, Oxfordshire, Wiltshire and Somerset. The northern and western edges are bounded by a steep incline, or escarpment, from where, on a clear day, walkers may be rewarded with spectacular views across the Severn Estuary and beyond to the Black Mountains in Wales. This escarpment is formed by the uplifting of the limestone layer that underlies the region, exposing its broken edge.

    It is this limestone that gives the area one of its most distinctive qualities – the warm honey-coloured building material that is found extensively in manor houses, cottages, churches, town halls, barns and walls. This characteristic Cotswold stone helps to unify a landscape that is otherwise diverse in nature, the open downlands, broad arable fields and grazing pastures with dry-stone walls contrasting with the intimate river valleys and dense woodlands, each habitat supporting its own variety of flora and fauna – dormice in hazel coppices, blue butterflies on limestone grasslands, kingfishers along the riverbanks. The landscape is criss-crossed by a network of public footpaths and long-distance paths, over

4,830km (3,000 miles) in all, including the 164km (102 mile) Cotswold Way that runs along the Cotswold escarpment from Chipping Campden to Bath, plus the Monarch's Way, Warden's Way and Windrush Way, all of which feature in this book. Such walks link the numerous small towns and villages scattered across the region, many of medieval origin dating back to the Domesday Book of 1086, with picture-postcard thatched cottages, archetypal village greens and historic churches. These villages help to give the area its distinctive character and charm, and combine with the rolling landscape to make the Cotswolds such a popular destination with walkers and tourists alike.

THE WALKS

The walks featured in this book cover a huge range of different landscapes and points of interest: several follow the escarpment (pages 28, 36, 40, 64 and 76), affording spectacular views in all directions; others pass along quiet river valleys (pages 44 and 52) or through peaceful farmland visiting picturesque villages (pages 72 and 84); and some explore ancient woods (page 60), nature reserves (pages 24 and 52) and deer parks (page 16). Wildlife features widely, with walks across some of Britain's most precious habitats: limestone grassland with its associated wild flowers and butterflies (pages 28) and ancient beech woodland carpeted with bluebells in May (page 64). Then there are the special-interest walks: seeking out deserted villages (page 44) and battle sites (page 56); exploring the industrial heritage of canals (page 68) and old flour and woollen mills (pages 72 and 80); and following in the footsteps of famous people, such as author Laurie Lee (page 24), designer William Morris (page 76) and King Charles II (page 48).

Many of the routes are waymarked, making them easy to follow, and nearly all are circular, with traditional country pubs along the way where you can stop off for some welcome refreshments. General advice on how to reach your starting point is provided, and although some areas are relatively remote it is always good to consider whether you can leave the car at home and take public transport (check online at www.traveline.org.uk before you go, especially as many bus services do not run on Sundays). Also provided are suggestions for local attractions that you may choose to visit after your walk, such as nearby gardens, country-house estates, Roman villas, railway museums and wildlife parks.

WALKING THE COTSWOLDS

- Many of the walks may be damp and muddy after rain, so always wear suitable footwear: walking shoes or boots are advisable.
- The maps in this book provide a good guide to the routes, but it is often handy to have an Ordnance Survey map with you when out walking, to supplement the maps provided.
- If you are walking alone, let someone know where you are and when you expect to return.
- Consider taking a mobile phone with you, bearing in mind coverage can be patchy in rural areas.
- Some of the walks take you along small country lanes without pavements. Always walk facing oncoming traffic (except when approaching a right-hand bend when it is advisable to cross the road for a clear view), keep children and dogs under close control, and wear something light or brightly coloured when visibility is poor (at dusk, for example).
- Take special care of children beside water, particularly alongside canals where the sides can be steep and the water deep.
- Support the rural economy by spending your money at local facilities, such as shops, cafés and pubs.
- While the author has taken every care to ensure the accuracy of this walking guide, changes to the routes may occur after publication. Where advised to do so at the end of the directions (that is, on the Cotswold Way National Trail walks on pages 28, 64 and 76), you should check the routes on the appropriate website before setting out.
- Public transport may also change over time, so if you are thinking of taking a bus to your destination, always check timetables and routes online or with local tourist information centres before setting out.

FOLLOW THE COUNTRYSIDE CODE

Here's how to respect, protect and enjoy the countryside:

- Always park sensibly, making sure that your vehicle is not blocking access to drives, fields and farm tracks.
- Leave gates as you find them or follow instructions on signs. If walking in a group, make sure the last person knows how to leave a gate.
- In fields where crops are growing, follow the paths wherever possible.
- Use gates, stiles or gaps in field boundaries when provided – climbing over walls, hedges and fences causes damage.
- Don't leave litter and leftover food – it not only spoils the beauty of the countryside but can be dangerous to wildlife and farm animals as well.
- Keep all dogs under strict control, particularly near livestock, and observe any requests to keep dogs on leads. (Remember, by law farmers are entitled to destroy a dog that injures or worries their animals.)
- Always clean up after your dog and get rid of the mess responsibly.
- Take special care not to damage, destroy or remove flowers, trees or even rocks: they provide homes and food for wildlife, and add to everybody's enjoyment of the countryside.
- Don't get too close to wild animals and farm animals as they can behave unpredictably.
- Be careful not to disturb ruins and historic sites.
- Be careful not to drop a match or smouldering cigarette at any time of the year, as this can cause fires.
- Get to know the signs and symbols used in the countryside. Visit the 'Finding your way' pages on Natural England's website for more information*.

* For full details of the countryside code, visit
www.naturalengland.org.uk/ourwork/enjoying/countrysidecode

Five Fields Walk

MILTON UNDER WYCHWOOD AND FIFIELD

*This 'Step into the Cotswolds' waymarked route
starts in the west Oxfordshire village of Milton under
Wychwood – an old village dating from medieval times. The
gently undulating route takes you across fields and streams, past
grazing sheep and hovering kestrels, to the village of Fifield,
mentioned in the Domesday Book of 1086. Its name probably derives
from its Anglo–Saxon name of Fifhides, meaning 'five hides' (a hide
being a field). From here you can extend your walk to take in Little
Rissington Airfield, an RAF aerodrome and former RAF station
built during the 1930s and once home to the Central Flying
School, the Red Pelicans and the Red Arrows.*

DISTANCE:	9.5km (6 miles) (circular) with 3km (2 miles) extension
TIME:	Allow 3–4 hours (with extension: 4–5 hours)
LEVEL:	Easy (with one short, steep section on extension route)
START/PARKING:	The Quart Pot public house at Milton under Wychwood (OX7 6LA), with on-street parking. OS grid reference SP263183 (OS Explorer map OL45)
GETTING THERE:	*By car:* Turn off A40 Oxford to Cheltenham Road at Burford on to A361 towards Chipping Norton; after about 6.5km (4 miles), bear left in Shipton-under-Wychwood to Milton-under-Wychwood. *By public transport:* Train to Kingham then bus no. X8 (or bus no. 233 Sunday, limited service)
REFRESHMENTS:	The Quart Pot or Wychwood Deli at Milton under Wychwood, or The Merrymouth Inn, Fifield
LOCAL ATTRACTIONS:	Foxholes Nature Reserve

DIRECTIONS

1. From The Quart Pot pub, turn left into Church Road heading towards Lyneham and Kingham. After 400m (440yd), opposite the turning to Lyneham, turn left through a gate into some allotments and immediately left again. At the corner turn right and walk straight on to the far side of the field.

2. At the far side of the field turn left and cross the footbridge to reach a gate. Cross the next field towards Breurn Grange, reaching a field gate by a garden wall. Bear slightly right to the corner of the garden then continue up to a gate and on to the lane.

3. Turn left up the lane. After approximately 130m (140yd) take the bridleway on the right marked 'Fifield 1'. Go diagonally left across the field to a gate. Once through the gate, turn right and follow the field edge to a gap in the hedge. Cross the footbridge and walk straight ahead alongside a stream.

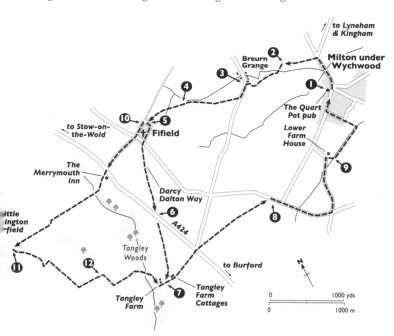

4. Where a bridge crosses the stream, turn left and go through the gate into the next field. Bear right across this field to a gate next to an electricity pole. Continue diagonally up the next field following the electricity poles to a bridlegate in the corner. Turn left and follow the edge of the playing field into Fifield.

5. If you wish to extend your walk to Little Rissington Airfield, go straight to direction 10 below. Otherwise, turn left and follow the lane round to the right and up to the church. At the top of the lane, turn left and then right on to the Darcy Dalton Way, following the path between a fence and hedge to a gate leading into a field. Continue diagonally across this field to a gap in the hedge. Bear left and follow the edge of the next field to another gate. Continue diagonally right across the next field to the A424.

6. Cross the road carefully then bear diagonally right across the next two fields before going through a gate. Continue across the next field before passing through a gate at the back of the farmhouse at Tangley Farm on to a lane.

7. Turn left and follow the farm track and lane leading uphill, past Tangley Farm Cottages, to the main road. Cross the road then almost immediately take the footpath on the right. Bear diagonally right across the next three fields using through-gaps in the hedges. At the far edge of the third field, pass through a gate and cut across the corner of the next field to another gate. Cross the paddock to a field gate on to the lane.

8. Turn right and follow the lane until you meet a crossroads. Here, turn left on to the lane marked 'Milton under Wychwood', then turn right on to a footpath beside Lower Farm House. Go straight ahead to a field gate and continue straight on across the field to a bridge.

9. After crossing the bridge turn left and follow the stream along the edge of the next three fields. Halfway along the third field turn left over a stone bridge, through a gate and straight on to a gate leading into Jubilee Lane. Follow Jubilee Lane then turn right into the High Street to return to The Quart Pot.

10. To extend the walk from point 5 on the map, turn right and follow the lane round to the left, carrying on until you reach the main road (A424). Cross this road and take the lane by the side of The Merrymouth Inn. Where the lane bears right by the farm, continue straight ahead down the restricted byway, following the track until you have almost reached the locked gate leading on to the airfield. The RAF station closed in 1994 and the airfield is now home to 637 Volunteer Gliding Squadron, which provides basic flying training for the Combined Cadet Force and Air Training Corps cadets.

11. Turn left before the gate and follow the hedge alongside the field. At the corner of the field turn left, then right and continue along the edge of the next field. At the far corner of the second field on the left, turn left and follow the track as it descends to a gate. Continue straight ahead and cross the bridge.

12. Shortly after crossing the stream, the bridleway bears right and climbs to a metal gate. Go straight on, between two hedges, and through a second gate on to a farm track. Follow this track to Tangley Farm, bearing left over the cattle grid to rejoin the walk at point 7 on the map (go to direction 7 above).

Courtesy of the Cotswolds Conservation Board. For more information see cotswoldsaonb.org.uk

GHOST OF A FOREST

Milton under Wychwood is named after the Royal Forest of Wychwood, which at the time of the Domesday Book in 1086 covered much of what is now west Oxfordshire. In 1854 an Act of Parliament was passed to clear the forest for agricultural land. In a period of only 18 months, thousands of trees were cut down and areas of woodland and heath were cleared, leaving only the present rump of woodland round Cornbury Park to the north-east of Leafield (see Cornbury Park Walk, page 16). In 1997 the Wychwood Project was established to raise awareness of the history and identity of the area, and to work with local communities to restore the rich patchwork of landscapes and habitats within the forest boundaries.

Cornbury Park Walk

CHARLBURY, FINSTOCK AND WYCHWOOD FOREST

*This delightful walk starts in the small market town
of Charlbury, a conservation area on the north-eastern edge of the
Cotswolds that was once an important centre for glove-making:
the last manufacturer closed here in the late 1960s. The walk takes
you through the Cornbury Park Estate, with its splendid 600-acre
deer park, and on to Wychwood Forest, now a National Nature
Reserve. Along the way you pass the village of Finstock,
where Queen Victoria's maid and close friend of 46 years –
Jane Spencer, Baroness Churchill – lies buried.*

DISTANCE:	13km (8 miles) (circular) or shorter route of 9km (5½ miles)
TIME:	Allow 4–5 hours (shorter route: 2½–3½ hours)
LEVEL:	Moderate
START/PARKING:	The library in Market Street, Charlbury (OX7 3PN). Park at Charlbury Station or Spendlove Centre, Eastone Road. OS grid reference SP356195 (OS Explorer map 191)
GETTING THERE:	By car: 9.5km (6 miles) south of Chipping Norton on B4026, and 22km (13½ miles) north-west of Oxford, following A44 through Woodstock, then turning left on to B4437 towards Charlbury *By public transport:* By train to Charlbury
REFRESHMENTS:	The Bull Inn, Charlbury, and The Crown Inn, Finstock
LOCAL ATTRACTIONS:	Blenheim Palace; North Leigh Roman Villa

DIRECTIONS

1. Known for its annual beer festival, Charlbury has changed little in the last 100 years or more and is well worth a visit before starting your walk. With your back to the library, walk to your left down Market Street, turn right into Church Street, then bear left into Park Street. After approximately 0.5km (⅓ mile) turn right down the lane to Cornbury Park, crossing over the railway line and the river. Once a royal hunting park, Cornbury is now owned by Lord Rotherwick and home to the annual Cornbury Festival – an eclectic, eccentric, family-oriented music carnival disguised as a country fayre.

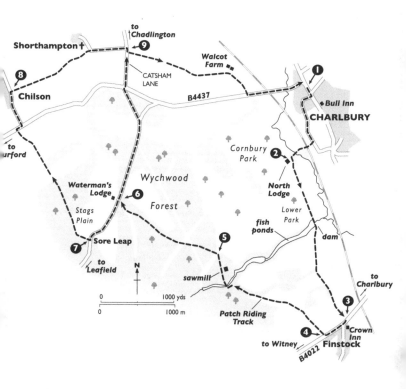

2. Upon reaching North Lodge turn immediately left, through the wooden door, and follow the footpath next to the fence line through Lower Park to some fish ponds. Now walk across the dam. On the other side bear right through the trees and follow the waymarked path along the tree-lined avenue before doglegging right and left on to a track. Bear left where the track forks and continue along the field edge to a gate. Bear right across Manor House gardens and go through a gap in the yew hedge to a stone stile beyond.

3. Cross the stile and turn right along the road verge into Finstock on the Witney/Charlbury road. The name Finstock means 'the place frequented by woodpeckers', a name that dates back to a time when Wychwood Forest covered much of this area; today, all that survives of Finstock's arboreal past is Topples Wood to the north-east of the village. Continue on past the lay-by until you reach a track off to the right that leads you into Wychwood Forest.

4. Follow the Patch Riding Track as it starts to descend downhill, passing a coppice and following an old stone wall. Follow the stone track signed to the left over a stile and carry on down the hill. Bear right at the lake and walk uphill past the sawmill, keeping to the path, and emerge on to an open grassy area with a wall beyond.

5. Take the clearly waymarked wide avenue uphill towards the Leafield road, taking care not to trample any plants growing on the path. Cross the stile opposite Waterman's Lodge.

6. Upon reaching the road you can either turn right, taking the short cut, or turn left and follow the longer route. For the short cut, continue along the road for about 1.5km (1 mile), then branch left at the fork, signed to Chadlington. Carry on to Catsham Lane and rejoin the walk at point 9 on the map, turning right on to the bridleway. For the longer route, walk left along the Leafield road until you reach the woodland at Sore Leap.

7. Take the footpath on the right, following the wood's edge, then bear right shortly afterwards across Stags Plain. Continue along the path into the woodland, crossing

Cornbury Park

First mentioned in the Domesday Book of 1086, Cornbury originated as a royal hunting park on the edge of Wychwood Forest. Historical records from 1337 make mention of payment for 'a stone wall about Cornbury Park [and] a house called 'Logge' of stone and timber'. In 1642 the park passed out of royal hands when Charles I gave it to the Earl of Danby 'forever'. Forever didn't last long, and by 1661 the park was owned by the first Earl of Clarendon (father-in-law to the future James II) who started to build the house we see today. Wychwood Forest forms part of the Cornbury Estate and is one of the few private forests in England. Its unique habitat contains some of Britain's most ancient broadleaved woodland, comprising mainly oak, ash and beech, with ground flora including meadow saffron, herb paris, early purple orchid and adder's tongue fern.

a couple of forestry tracks until you emerge from the woods on the far side. Cross the fields heading towards Chilson village until you reach the main Burford/Charlbury road. Turn right and then left on to a lane that takes you down into the village.

8. Halfway through Chilson village take the bridleway marked to the right. Follow the path through the hamlet of Shorthampton, taking time, if possible, to make a slight detour to view the humble 12th-century church with its traces of medieval wall painting. Continue down the lane until you reach Catsham Lane. Turn right and then left on to the bridleway.

9. Continue to follow the bridleway signed to Charlbury, passing through Walcot Farm and on until you reach the main road. Turn left into Charlbury, passing the station, a listed building designed by Isambard Kingdom Brunel. Turn right into Market Street to take you back to your starting point.

Courtesy of Oxfordshire County Council. For similar walks see www.oxfordshire.gov.uk/walksandrides or www.oxfordshirecotswolds.org/walks

Oxfordshire Ramble

CHIPPING NORTON, SALFORD AND CORNWELL

*This delightful walk takes you across gently undulating
countryside, through kissing gates, fields and farmyards, from
the market town of Chipping Norton to the Cotswold villages of
Salford and Cornwell. Known as 'the Gateway to the Cotswolds',
Chipping Norton is the highest town in Oxfordshire and is
situated on the western slopes of a hillside that was once the site of
a Norman castle. The route takes you close by Bliss Mill with its
distinctive tall chimney, which is a landmark for miles around.
Here, high-quality tweed was made for many years. The mill
finally closed in 1980 and has now been converted
into luxury apartments.*

DISTANCE:	10km (6½ miles) (circular)
TIME:	Allow 3½–4½ hours
LEVEL:	Easy
START/PARKING:	Crown and Cushion Hotel on Chipping Norton High Street (OX7 5AD), parking in New Street car park off the A44, just west of town. OS grid reference SP314272 (OS Explorer map OL45)
GETTING THERE:	*By car:* On A44, midway between Oxford and Evesham *By public transport:* By train to Kingham, then take bus no. X8 to Chipping Norton (limited Sunday service)
REFRESHMENTS:	Numerous pubs, cafés and restaurants in Chipping Norton, also The Black Horse in Salford
LOCAL ATTRACTIONS:	The Rollright Stones; Sezincote House and Garden

DIRECTIONS

1. From The Crown and Cushion Hotel on Chipping Norton High Street, cross over the street, bear right and then turn immediately left down Goddards Lane with the Blue Boar pub on your right-hand side. Walk past The Chequers pub, cross over into Church Street and walk down into St Mary's churchyard. Cross the churchyard, bearing left on the path ahead, and exit past the white wooden gate.

2. When the path opens up, enter the recreation ground at the first kissing gate. Walk diagonally across the field to the far corner, skirting around the play area on the left to the kissing gate, down the slope and over the concrete bridge at the bottom.

3. Over the bridge the footpath forks in two – take the left-hand path directly up the slope in front of you. Proceed through the two kissing gates either side of the road and on to the tarmac path at the edge of the cemetery. Exit the cemetery via another kissing gate.

4. On the opposite side of the tarmac road are two fields divided by a wide hedge. Cross over the road and walk along the right-hand side of the hedge. Exit the field at the top left corner and follow the path ahead as it crosses the large field. Exit this field via the kissing gate and walk on the right of the hedge in the next field.

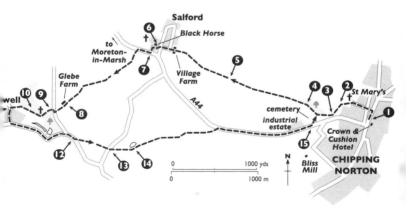

21

5. Once you have walked approximately halfway through this field, you will come across a gap in the hedge with a kissing gate. Go through the gate and, bearing right, head for the gate at the bottom of this field. Once through, proceed in the same direction and through the next gate. Continue on the wider footpath and eventually through two gates close together to enter Village Farm. Walk straight ahead between the farm buildings and you will come out on a bend in a road. Go straight on towards the village. At the next junction bear left, with the village hall on your right.

6. Walk through the village for around 90m (100yd) to the next T-junction. Follow the path as it curves to the right and cross over. Walk along the gravel path towards the church (signed 'Church'). Do not follow the path as it bends into the church or cross the cattle grid into the field ahead. Instead turn left and follow the waymarked path at the field boundary.

7. When you reach the A44, turn right and walk a short distance on the right side of the road. You will shortly see a bridleway on the opposite side of the road. Carefully cross over and follow the bridleway for about 0.8km (½ mile).

8. Entering Glebe Farm, follow the bridleway left and then right between the farm buildings. Exit the farm along a drive towards the road. Turn right at the road and very shortly cross over and take the first footpath on the left.

9. Continue along the path as it goes down the dip, over a bridge and straight up the other side. You will shortly approach a church. Go through the metal kissing gate, follow the path through the churchyard and exit in the far right corner. Proceed along the tree-lined concrete walkway ahead.

10. Halfway along the walkway there is a kissing gate on the right signed 'Darcy Dalton Way'. Go through the gate and follow the path as it heads off left towards the open field. When the field opens up you will see another kissing gate on your left, again signed 'Darcy Dalton Way'. Go through the gate and immediately turn right. Walk diagonally through the orchard, to join a track.

11. Follow the track to the T-junction with a road. Turn left again and follow the road through the village of Cornwell. You will eventually walk up to another T-junction at which you should turn left.

12. Follow the road for approximately 1km (¾ mile) until you come to a small junction with a road on the left. At the junction take the bridleway across the field. After the first field, continue straight ahead with the hedge-line of the next field on your right. Exit via a gate, cross the minor road and go through another gate into the field ahead.

13. The large open field has a fenced-off pond in the middle. Walk across the field, skirting around the right of the pond, and exit over the bridge in the corner.

14. You will enter the next field in a corner with two paths ahead. Follow the left path as it leads up to the far corner. Exit the field via the gate and on to the next footpath. Follow the tree- and hedge-lined footpath and you will come out on a drive. Continue straight on to the A44. Turn right and walk towards Chipping Norton.

15. When the first residential area peters out, cross over and turn left into the industrial estate. Walk straight ahead and past the Owen Mumford building on your right. You will eventually find a kissing gate on your right, which you have been through before. Go through the gate into the cemetery. Retrace your steps through the cemetery, using directions 3, 2 and 1 to return to your starting point.

Courtesy of the Cotswolds Conservation Board.
For more information see www.cotswoldsaonb.org.uk

THE CURIOUS CASE OF CORNWELL

At first glance, Cornwell looks like a typical Cotswold village, with its honey-coloured cottages and mullioned windows. But look closer and you soon realize it is slightly different from the other limestone villages that surround it, with more than its fair share of idiosyncratic details such as the oversized ball finials on the gate posts and the chunky buttressing on the cottages. This is thanks to Clough Williams-Ellis, the famed architect of the Welsh village of Portmeirion, who restored Cornwell in the 1930s, along with the nearby manor house. Of particular note is the extraordinary village hall, with its stepped bell tower and apsidal (curved) end.

'Cider With Rosie' Walk

The Slad Valley

*This walk passes through one of England's most beautiful
areas, immortalised in the charming book* Cider With Rosie
*by local author Laurie Lee. It links three of the Gloucestershire
Wildlife Trust's finest nature reserves, where the flora and fauna
is still as rich as when Laurie Lee first roamed the countryside.
The route mainly follows waymarked public footpaths, crossing
stiles and babbling brooks, passing through fields and ancient
woodlands, and opening up from time to time to give spectacular
views across the valley. Look out for buzzards circling overhead
on sunny days, and any one of the 13 species of orchid
to be found on Swift's Hill.*

DISTANCE:	12km (7½ miles) (circular) or shorter route of 8km (5 miles)
TIME:	Allow 3½–4½ hours (shorter route: 2–3 hours)
LEVEL:	Quite demanding, with one very steep stretch
START/PARKING:	About 0.8km (½ mile) to the north of Slad Village, on the B4070 (nearby postcode: GL6 7QA); park in long lay-by opposite Bulls Cross Common. OS grid reference SO875085 (OS Explorer map 179)
GETTING THERE:	*By car:* 4.5km (3 miles) from Stroud on the B4070. Go through Slad Village until Frith Wood above you on left merges with the road. Continue over the junction to Bull Cross Common
REFRESHMENTS:	The Woolpack in Slad village
LOCAL ATTRACTIONS:	Painswick Rococo Garden; Countryside Centre
NOTE:	Land is privately owned, so please stay on the public footpath

DIRECTIONS

1. From the lay-by, walk along the roadside, away from Slad, for about 100m (110yd) until you come to a public footpath on your right (note: do not take the path to Trillgate Farm). Follow the footpath down past a disused quarry on your left, noting the fine old pollarded beech trees. Upon reaching the gate, squeeze through (keeping dogs on a lead in this wood) and follow the waymarked track, bearing right through mostly conifer plantation.

2. Before reaching the lake, turn right off the track on to a smaller waymarked footpath, descending to the Slad Brook which was dammed to form the lake. The path can be very muddy here. From the brook carry on uphill, over the next track and straight up the steeply sloping path ahead of you (the toughest part of the walk).

3. At the top, go over the stile and on to the track. Cross the track diagonally left to another stile in the stone wall. From here there are wonderful views across the Slad Valley. Follow the well-worn path down across the field to the hedge and along to the corner where you enter Snow's Farm Nature Reserve.

4. The route through the reserve is waymarked with red arrows. From the entrance follow the arrows left down through the woodland, then turn right just past The Old Shop, over a stile and right again. Follow the arrows along the nearer, south-facing side of the valley, walking along narrow sheep paths across the fields, and passing through scrub, hedges, gates and a wooded area (watch out for hidden rabbit holes!). Gradually descend and go through a small gate before crossing the Dillay Brook near the hut and information board. Then go through a second gate and turn right to the exit kissing gate.

5. Walk briefly down a muddy slope and, before the stream, go left and over the stile. Follow the waymark to the right and cross over a stream by the plank (beware: this can be slippery when wet). Continue up the slope and over the next stile, heading towards Catswood on the worn path. On reaching the wood look back for the fine views across the valley. Cross the stile into Catswood, an ancient woodland of mainly ash, beech and hazel. Turn right and follow the muddy track along the woodland edge. Pass through the metal gate and stay on the track as it bears around to the left (don't fork left or right). The track is joined by a hollow way (King Charles' Lane) coming up from the right. Shortly afterwards fork left and you soon reach Catswood Lane.

6. Follow the lane down to the right with Dunkitehill Wood on your left. Further on you reach the signed track to Furners Farm on your right. If you wish to take the shorter route, go down this track and rejoin the walk at point 9 on the map (go straight to direction 9, below). Otherwise carry on past the farm track, rounding a sharp left-hand bend to reach the hamlet of Elcombe. Continue along beneath Trantershill Plantation until you come to the Elliot Nature Reserve at Swift's Hill.

7. Near the information board take the track up to the left, passing the disused quarry on your right. Bear right at the top, keeping the hedge/fence on your left. From the 'summit', you can either take the well-worn path on the right straight down the hill, or carry on to the lower path that begins at the eastern point, beside Abbey Wood.

8. Upon reaching the information board, turn left on to the lane and go down the hill, past Knapp Farm. At a sharp left turn in the lane turn off to the right at a footpath sign (which also marks Upper Vatch Mill), and on to a track with conifers on you left. After 25m (27yd) cross the waymarked stile on the right, and walk left through the field. Cross another stile and follow the worn path towards Furners Farm, crossing more stiles and a small dam and bearing right through the field. Emerge on to the track, turning left towards the farm.

9. At the farm, turn right between the cottages and farm buildings, and straight on through the farm gate. Continue across the fields, below the hedge/fence and into a dense blackthorn thicket. Cross the stile immediately in front and go through a small beech coppice. Walk down the left side of the field and cross the stile into Steanbridge Lane near the Bridge Pond (a mill pond).

10. Turn left up the tarmac lane, then sharp right on to a tiny lane that leads round to the main road by the war memorial. Opposite the memorial is the lane leading to Frith Wood Nature Reserve.

11. Enter the wood by the information board and follow the lower woodland edge for a short way before bearing uphill on the bridleway, marked by blue spots on trees. At the top you reach the main bridleway which runs along the ridge. Turn right, passing another information board, and carry on to the exit to Bulls Cross Common. Cross the B4070 and head back to the lay-by.

Courtesy of Gloucestershire Wildlife Trust. For more information about the wildlife on this walk go to www.gloucestershirewildlifetrust.co.uk/reserves

Cleeve Hill Common Ring

*Incorporating part of the Cotswold Way as it traverses
Cleeve Hill – at 330m (1,083ft) the highest point in the
Cotswolds – this breathtaking walk leads you over open hilltops,
across streams and through woodlands, immersing you in one of
the country's most fascinating and precious habitats: limestone
grassland. Sitting atop the Cotswold escarpment, on what is
often called the Cotswold Edge, and containing a Site of Special
Scientific Interest (SSSI), the area is rich in butterflies, birds
and wild flowers, and provides unsurpassed views of the
surrounding countryside, reaching as far as Wales
on a clear day.*

DISTANCE:	9.5km (6 miles) (circular) or shorter route of 6.5km (4 miles)
TIME:	Allow 3–4 hours (shorter route: 2–3 hours)
LEVEL:	Moderate, with some steep sections (shorter route is easy)
START/PARKING:	By Cleeve Hill village, in the quarry car park across the track from Cleeve Hill Golf Club (GL52 3PW). OS grid reference SO989272 (OS Explorer map 179)
GETTING THERE:	*By car:* From Cheltenham, take the B4632 towards Winchcome, turning right at the signpost to Cleeve Hill Golf Club; the quarry car park is just beyond the club entrance *By public transport:* Train to Cheltenham, then bus no. 606 Cheltenham/Winchcombe to golf course junction (not Sundays)
REFRESHMENTS:	Bar café/restaurant at the golf club
LOCAL ATTRACTIONS:	Belas Knap Long Barrow (English Heritage)

DIRECTIONS

1. Leave the car park and turn right to follow the track down around the bottom of the hill. As a wonderful view of Winchcombe nestled in its valley opens up to your left, carry on following the Cotswold Way down through two metal field gates.

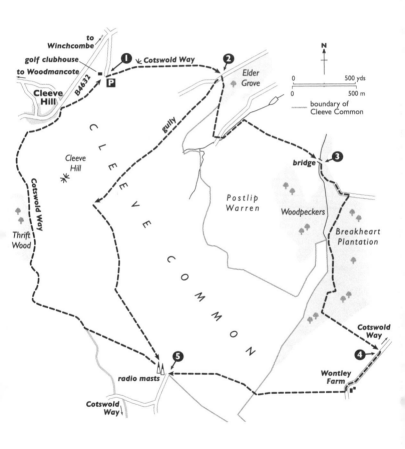

2. For a shorter route that avoids the steep climbs but doesn't miss out on the views, turn right immediately after the second gate to leave the Cotswold Way and follow the track around the bottom of the hill. Continue all the way along the side of the gully, eventually turning left on to the wider track at the top. Head straight across the common and make directly for the radio masts at the end to rejoin the route at point 5 on the map (go straight to direction 5 below). Otherwise, follow the Cotswold Way down towards the trees and through the gate at the bottom, past the farm buildings and through a few more gates. Once you meet the road at the end, turn left and continue uphill, past the houses on your left. Continue through to the end of the farmyard, and take the gate on your left, turning right downhill towards the stream at the bottom.

3. At any time of the year, the shade of the woodlands and the calming sound of peacefully flowing water make this little bridge the ideal spot to stop and rest awhile before the climbs ahead. When you are ready, cross over the bridge and follow the trail up to the right. At the top pass through the gate and across the paddock, turning right when you meet the road. Carry on past the stable, and continue to follow the signs through the woods. After the steep climb snaking up the wooded hillside, a kissing gate is well placed on which to lean and catch your breath. Keep on following the Cotswold Way to the end of the woods and along the edge of an open field, until you reach a kissing gate and fingerpost at the far side.

4. Leaving the Cotswold Way behind for the time being, turn right and follow the unmade road down towards the deserted farm buildings. Immediately afterwards, turn right through the gateway and follow the path slowly uphill through the fields towards the radio masts in the distance. Pass through a gate back on to the common and take the path on the right towards the waymark post, and continue to head for the masts.

Birds and Butterflies

With their rich flora, limestone grasslands are ideal places to look for butterflies: here you will find dark-green fritillary, chalkhill blue, small heath, dingy skipper and brown argus butterflies – all characteristic of high-quality grasslands. Birds are also abundant: in springtime look out for wheatears, skylarks, meadow pipits, stonechats and willow warblers. If you're lucky you might spot a grasshopper warbler in the low gorse patches, and if you're luckier still you could see something even rarer, such as the ring ouzel or great grey shrike. In the summer look out for skylarks, stonechats, whitethroats and meadow pipits or possibly a wandering red kite; in winter you may see large flocks of winter thrushes (fieldfares and redwings), along with finch flocks and ravens.

5. At the masts, turn right to follow the fence line until you meet the Cotswold Way. Continue right along the edge of the escarpment, benefiting from some of the finest views in England. Limestone grasslands such as these are particularly rich in wild flowers, including nationally rare species such as musk orchid, purple milk-vetch, bastard-toadflax, limestone fern and flat sedge. Adders and common lizards are also to be found. To return to your starting point, follow the path over the golf course and down towards the reward awaiting you at the clubhouse. A rest at the end of your walk is a chance to plan your next trip!

Courtesy of the Natural England/Cotswold Way National Trail. For updated information on this walk and for similar walks see www.nationaltrail.co.uk/Cotswold

Bath Skyline Walk

*Set in the southern edge of the Cotswolds, this picturesque
walk allows you to savour the magnificent views down on to the
World Heritage City of Bath while strolling through the peace
of hidden valleys, tranquil woodlands and patchworks of small
meadows, all rich in wildlife. In spring and summer colourful wild
flowers can be seen all around and the pungent smell of wild garlic
is never far away. The route follows the waymarked path, with
some steep climbs, but there are plenty of other footpaths that
cross level ground and detour around some of the steeper hills.
Other detours allow you to explore an 18th-century folly
and an ancient hill fort.*

DISTANCE:	9.5km (6 miles) (circular)
TIME:	Allow 3–4 hours
LEVEL:	Moderate, with some steep climbs
START/PARKING:	Beside RSPCA Cats and Dogs Home, Claverton Down (BA2 7AZ). Park-and-ride available on Saturdays at university, otherwise only limited roadside parking. OS Grid reference BA773641 (OS Explorer map 155)
GETTING THERE:	*By car:* Bath is just off the A4 Bath–Bristol and A36 Bath–Warminster routes, and is 26km (16 miles) from junction 18 on the M4 *By public transport:* By train to Bath Spa, then bus no. 18 or 418 to Bath University; or 1.5km (1 mile) walk from city centre, up fairly steep hill, joining the Skyline Walk at point 6 on the map
REFRESHMENTS:	Light refreshments in Widcombe and Combe Down or a variety of restaurants, cafés and pubs in Bath
LOCAL ATTRACTIONS:	Bath – UNESCO World Heritage site; Prior Park Landscape Garden (National Trust)

DIRECTIONS

1. Standing in front of the RSPCA home, facing the University, turn right and go over a stone stile built into the wall on the left. Follow the path right, through a gate, and turn left on to a track. Follow the track to the corner of the field, through the kissing gate, and then cross diagonally to the far corner. Continue straight on, following the path along the wooded edge of the next field.

2. When you reach the far end of the field follow the path through Bathampton Woods. When the path forks, bear left and keep to the main path as it meanders through the wood.

3. At the edge of the woods continue straight on, crossing a track. Bear left and climb slightly to walk along the top of the slope, keeping the scrub immediately below you to your right. Bear right at a wall and proceed downhill to where the path meets Bathwick Woods. Follow the path along the top edge of the woodland and then gradually move away from the woodland to join a track near the television masts. Follow this track until you reach the second kissing gate on your right.

4. Follow the path steeply downhill through the woodland. Just before a fence turn left and follow the path as it contours round the slope though the woodland, then out by some railings just before the stone pillars of the golf club drive. (From here you can take a detour to the 18th-century folly known as Sham Castle). Go through the kissing gate on the right of the stone pillars and follow the path downhill, keeping the field boundary on your left.

5. At the kissing gate cross the road with care and turn right along the pavement. Continue to a footpath off to left and follow it downhill to emerge from between houses on to Cleveland Walk. Turn left and continue until the road meets Bathwick Hill. Cross over the busy T-junction with care to join a path leading between the houses opposite.

6. Follow the path to reach a field behind the houses. Go through the kissing gate and bear left, then cross the field diagonally into the next field. Carry straight on, through the kissing gate, on to another kissing gate and across the next field. Cross a small footbridge and turn right, following the path downhill, then down some steps to join a track. Go straight on along the track, past Smallcombe Farm, and enter the field opposite the gateway to the farm track.

7. Bear right, walking diagonally uphill across the field, then diagonally across the next field. At the far corner turn immediately right to meet the main road. Turn left and follow the road uphill to the footpath on the right. Cross the road and follow the footpath steeply uphill to the kissing gate at the far end. Turn right and follow the path, keeping the boundary of the field to your right. Go through the gap in the wall at the corner of the field and carry straight on along the track for approximately 100m (110yd). Then bear right, away from the gravel path and towards a gap in the nearby trees.

8. Cross the tarmac path and follow the steps downhill alongside the railings. At the bottom turn left along the path, keeping the railings on your right. Follow the path as it bears left uphill to reach the playing fields. Turn right and, keeping the fence on your left, walk around the end of the field to the kissing gate on the far side. Cross the cycle path and continue to the next kissing gate. Follow the path through the woodland, across a private driveway and along the edge of the woodland. The path continues along the field edge for a short distance and then re-enters the woodland. Follow the path to the right, around an old quarry. At the edge of the woodland turn left to reach a kissing gate that takes you into a field.

9. Follow the path along the right edge of the field to two kissing gates. Go through the right-hand gate and follow the path along a wall and then between two fences to reach the main road. Turn left along the road and take a footpath on the right. Follow this along the edge of the field, keeping the boundary immediately to your left, until you get back to the RSPCA home.

Courtesy of The National Trust. For similar walks go to www.nationaltrust.org.uk/walks

FOLLIES, QUARRIES AND FORTS

A small detour just before the stone pillars of the golf club drive (see direction 4) will lead you to Sham Castle, an 18th-century folly commissioned by Bath philanthropist Ralph Allen to give employment to local stonemasons and improve the view from Allen's home in Lilliput Alley. In Roman times, stones from the nearby quarry were transported along the route of Sham Castle Lane to be used in the building of Bath. Slightly to the east lies Bathampton Down Hill Fort, now believed to have been a cattle enclosure rather than a defensive fort. The large stones with holes in them scattered across the landscape are glacial deposits that were stood on end in the 18th century, possibly to mark out a racecourse.

Wotton to Waterloo

WOTTON-UNDER-EDGE CIRCULAR WALK

*This lovely walk along the Cotswold escarpment is full of
contrasts and provides a fine outlook over Wotton-Under-Edge
from all directions. The route takes you through the historic town –
well worth exploring if you have time – then briefly follows the
Cotswold Way along a meandering stream before climbing
steeply up Coombe Hill, from where you get impressive views.
It continues through Conygre Wood, again linking up with the
Cotswold Way to reach Wotton Hill with its landmark trees
and tremendous panoramic views. Further on, the walk
levels out, passing through fields and farms before
climbing back to Wotton.*

DISTANCE:	9km (5½ miles) (circular)
TIME:	Allow 2½–3½ hours
LEVEL:	Moderate, with some steep climbs
START/PARKING:	Park in the main car park in The Chipping (old market place, GL12 7AD). OS grid reference ST755932 (OS Explorer map 167)
GETTING THERE:	*By car:* 8km (5 miles) from junction 14 on the M5. From Nailsworth, take the B4058 *By public transport:* Train to Stroud, then take bus no. 40 to Wotton-Under-Edge (not Sundays) or Yate bus no. 627
REFRESHMENTS:	The White Lion or The Falcon Inn, Wotton-Under-Edge
LOCAL ATTRACTIONS:	Newark Park (National Trust)

DIRECTIONS

1. Leave the car park at the lowest corner along Rope Walk. Turn right into Long Street, down past the shops, and follow the road as it bends left into Church Street. It's worth stopping to have a look at the Perry and Dawes Almshouses through the archway on the right, noting the lovely stained-glass window in the chapel. At the bottom, turn left along the narrow path and after a few metres turn right into a factory yard. Cross this and go over a footbridge, then turn left on to the path alongside the stream.

2. On meeting the road turn right and follow the Cotswold Way along the stream path. Upon reaching the lane, turn right and immediately left, again following the stream alongside a field and on to the lane. As the lane bends up to the right at the end of the houses, go straight into the field through the small gate and follow the left boundary to the far corner. Turn right up the field to the corner and cross over the stile on to the road. Here you may sit on the old bench (dating from 1902) to get some great views. Now turn left along the main road to the corner.

3. Cross the road with care, looking out for traffic. Go up the enclosed lane and after a few metres cross the stile on the right into the field. Head up the field, keeping the old tree line on your left, and climb up to the stile in the top fence. Cross the second stile and turn left, and after a short walk bear right up a narrow path which climbs steadily around and up the hill. Where it opens out climb to the electricity pole on the skyline. Follow the hedge on the right to a gate and stile. Continue through the wood, ignoring the path down to the left, and where the track bears right fork left along the footpath to reach the Old London Road.

4. Turn sharply downhill and at the left bend go up the steps on the right to a gate. Follow the delightful path through Conygre Wood. After a while you will pass a building up on the right; after a similar distance, as the path climbs a little, look out for a stile and signpost on the right and leave the wood. Turn left along the road and soon turn right up the bridleway. At the junction of the paths, turn a sharp left and follow the Cotswold Way along the field edge to a gate on the right, then walk down to the walled clump of trees on Wotton Hill, originally planted in honour of the Battle of Waterloo. From the top of the hill, on a clear day, you can see as far as the towers of the Severn Estuary suspension bridge, the Black Mountains in Wales and the Mendip Hills south of Bristol. After enjoying the wide views, circle to your left and look for the Cotswold Way leaving the hill. Follow the route down until you reach the main B4060. (You could take a short cut back to the Wotton here by turning left along the road – see map).

5. Carefully cross the road, then turn right and after a few metres take the footpath on the left between the cottages (just after number 26). Turn right down the road then, just before the bollards, go left. At the bottom of this path cross Bradley Green, following the footpath sign for Bushford Bridge. Follow the left-hand hedge to a stile, then cross the next field diagonally to a gate. Continue with the boundary on you right to a stile on to the road. Turn left and walk down to the junction. Note the castellated former toll house.

6. Cross the road and follow the farm drive opposite. This path goes over a stile by the gate and along over another stile into Hopyard farmyard. Go out through the left gate on to the track. Continue via a series of gates and stiles. Nearing Kingswood, look out for a stile to the left of a gate that takes you on to the main Wotton road opposite a large house.

7. Turn right then left into Vineyard Lane. After 0.4km (¼ mile), as the lane turns right by some houses, turn left on to a track. Go over the stile into the field and cross to the stile and gate on the far side. Continue across the next field, keeping to the right of Haw Park Farm. Go over the next stile, keeping to the right of the field, and turn right over a stile, halfway up the hill. Immediately turn left uphill, through a gap in the old hedge. Go straight across the next field and over a stile on to a wide grassy path near a school playing field. When you reach the road opposite, you'll find the car park up to the left.

Courtesy of South Cotswold Ramblers. For more
information go to www.southcotswoldramblers.org.uk

THE WATERLOO PLANTATION

On Wotton Hill, high above Wotton-Under-Edge, stands a solitary group of trees, planted on the site of what was once a warning beacon, used to warn of the approach of the Spanish Armada in 1588. The original trees were planted in 1815 in commemoration of the Battle of Waterloo, but by the 1850s they had become thin and were felled for a bonfire. A beacon was once again lit in 1887, one of a chain that spanned the country in celebration of Queen Victoria's Golden Jubilee, after which the trees were replanted and enclosed in the stone wall you see today. These trees were replaced once more in 1952.

Historic Winchcombe Walk

WINCHCOMBE AND BELAS KNAP

Following a clearly marked 'Made for Walking' route, this delightful walk starts in the historic town of Winchcombe and takes you past the famous Sudeley Castle. From here you follow the Windrush Way along a small valley, then head west for the steep climb up the Cotswold escarpment, for spectacular views across Gloucestershire. If you choose, you can extend your walk to the top of the hill and visit Belas Knap, one of the great burial mounds of ancient Britain. The return route takes you back downhill, through meadows and kissing gates, to your starting point.

DISTANCE:	8km (5 miles) (circular) with 1.5km (1 mile) extension
TIME:	Allow 2½–3½ hours
LEVEL:	Moderate, with some climbing
START/PARKING:	Back Lane car park, Winchcombe (GL54 5PZ). OS grid reference SP023284 (OS Explorer map OL45)
GETTING THERE:	*By car:* Off B4632 Cheltenham to Broadway Road
	By public transport: Train to Cheltenham, then bus no. 606 from Cheltenham towards Broadway (not Sundays)
REFRESHMENTS:	The White Hart, Winchcombe
LOCAL ATTRACTIONS:	Sudeley Castle; Winchcombe Railway Museum

DIRECTIONS

1. With your back to the library, walk to the left side of the car park and follow the blue sign to the town centre. On reaching the High Street, turn left and

immediately right, down Castle Street. Descend the road and cross the River Isbourne. Cross to the right side of the road and take the footpath to the left of the Sudeley Castle Country Cottages sign. Climb to a kissing gate and enter the castle parkland.

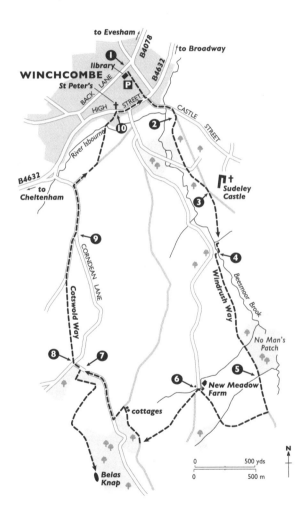

2. Follow the well-used route across the meadow. Go towards the right-hand fence, passing through a kissing gate, and turn left to descend to a road by two field gates. Go through the wooden right-hand gate and follow the yellow waymarks, keeping the fence on your left, with an elaborate children's play area beyond.

3. When level with the castle the path splits. Veer right towards a waymarked pole, passing a tree with a seat. Follow the well-used waymarked route (a green-and-white circle on a waymark indicates the Windrush Way). Descend the second low ridge to a bridge over a ditch, then veer right and then left to another kissing gate (this area can be wet). Bear right over another stream and turn left before the road.

4. Follow the fingerpost on your right signed 'Public Footpath Windrush Way'. Go through a field gate and veer away from the left-hand boundary – aim for a wooden power pole in the middle distance. Go over the stile to the left of a field gate and follow the track towards the right-hand corner of some woodland. In the corner of the field cross the double plank bridge and stile, keeping close to the fence and woodland on your left as you cross the next two fields.

5. Go over a stile beside a metal field gate and descend a gully to a stile on the far side of a small stream. Climb away from the stream and cross the centre of a field on a well-defined track. On reaching a gravel track on the far side of the field turn right at the sign 'Road used as a Public Path'. Stay on this track for 400m (440yd) until you reach some houses.

6. Turn left before the cream-coloured house, through a field gate with another sign 'Road used as a Public Path'. Follow the grass track up the hill, passing through a gate, for about 400m (440yd) and on reaching some woodland turn right through a field gate on to a gravel track. After passing some cottages turn left uphill to a road. Turn right following the Cotswold Way sign and continue along the narrow country road for about 400m (440yd).

7. On reaching the sign for Belas Knap it is well worth making an uphill detour to see this Bronze Age long barrow. Belas Knap is one of the great burial mounds of Britain, containing four burial chambers that housed 30 Bronze Age skeletons. Here, ancient chieftans were laid in their stone beds, and today the barrow looks much as it would have done 4,000 years ago. Upon returning to point 7 on the map, continue along the road to a T-junction.

8. At the T-junction, climb the bank ahead to a stone stile. Cross and take the right-hand path (signed 'Winchcombe 1¼ miles'), descending across the meadow on a well-used route. At the bottom of the hill cross a stile on to a road, turn right and continue until you reach another road.

9. Turn left on to the road and at a slight bend take the footpath signed on your right, going through the left hand of two kissing gates into a meadow with a clear view of Winchcombe church ahead. Aim for the church, then on reaching the hedge follow the boundary to a sports field, keeping the latter on your left until you reach a kissing gate. Go through and then exit the field between two stone pillars. Cross a bridge over the River Isbourne. Continue on the tarmac path between a hedge and a wall. As the wall ends, turn left and after 20m (22yd) turn right up another narrow path with walls on both sides.

10. Cross the High Street and turn left if you want to visit St Peter's Church. The church displays an altar cloth worked by Catherine of Aragon, the first wife of Henry VIII, and has 40 gargoyles, said to represent local town characters from the 1460s. Otherwise turn right along the raised footpath and at Cowl Lane turn left to the car park.

Courtesy of Tewkesbury Borough Council (www.tewkesbury.gov.uk).
For similar 'Made for Walking' walks ring 01684 855040.

A Well-Connected Castle

Built in 1442, Sudeley Castle has royal connections that date back hundreds of years, belonging variously to Edward IV, Richard III and eventually Henry VIII, who visited it with Anne Boleyn in 1535. Henry VIII's sixth wife and widow, Katherine Parr, lies buried in St Mary's Chapel at Sudeley. Elizabeth I visited on several occasions, and Charles I briefly made it his headquarters during the English Civil War, but in 1649 the castle was largely destroyed by Parliamentarians. A romantic ruin by the 18th century, the castle was finally restored in the 1840s by brothers John and William Dent – wealthy glovemakers whose name lives on to this day.

Windrush Valley Walk

ASTHALL, WIDFORD, SWINBROOK AND WORSHAM

*This classic Cotswold walk takes you through the fascinating
Windrush Valley – one of the most beautiful riverscapes in the
Cotswolds – past Norman churches and Italianate gardens,
through a deserted medieval village, and across the site of a
Roman road. Add to the mix some quaint riverside country pubs,
leafy lanes, grassy meadows alive with birdsong, and the sound
of leather on willow, and you have the essence of a quintessential
English summer. The walk starts in the pretty village of Asthall,
near Burford, once home to the notorious Mitford sisters who
amused and shocked society in equal measure during the 1930s.*

DISTANCE:	8km (5 miles) (circular) or 13.5km (8½ miles) with extension
TIME:	Allow 2½–3½ hours (4–5 hours with extension)
LEVEL:	Easy
START/PARKING:	Asthall village (OX18 4HW); a small amount of parking available. (Alternative parking can be found in Burford: see direction 8 for walk extension.) OS grid reference SP288113 (OS Explorer map OL45)
GETTING THERE:	*By car:* Turn off A40 Cheltenham to Oxford Road east of Burford on to B4047, then turn immediately left to Asthall *By public transport:* From Burford, take bus no.853 from the A40 lay-by and ask for the Asthall turn (very limited service)
REFRESHMENTS:	The Maytime Inn, Asthall or The Swan Inn, Swinbrook
LOCAL ATTRACTIONS:	Cotswold Wildlife Park; Minster Lovell Hall and Dovecote

DIRECTIONS

1. With your back to The Maytime Inn, turn right and follow the road past the church. Turn right at the T-junction and walk the 1.5km (1 mile) or so along the road to Widford, following the river to your right. Look out for the pollarded willows that line the Windrush near Asthall. Willow used to be an

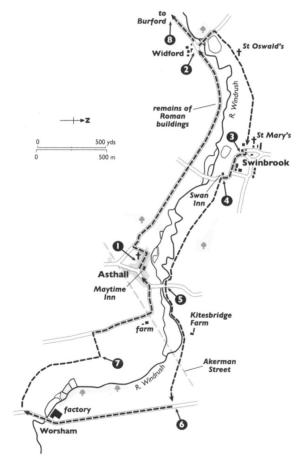

important crop for farmers, the branches being used for gate hurdles and the thinner ends for thatching pegs. As you approach Widford the road veers to the left and you pass some remains of Roman buildings, a sign that the whole of this part of the Windrush Valley was farmed in Romano–British times.

2. Turn right at Widford, crossing the two stone bridges, then turn right again along the footpath to Swinbrook, passing St Oswald's Church on your left. This tiny and tranquil church dates back to the 12th century and contains some interesting 14th-century murals. It was built on the site of a Roman villa – if you take time to visit it you can see fragments of mosaic flooring in the chancel. The uneven ground in the field surrounding the church is all that remains of the medieval village of Widford, which was deserted partly as a result of the Black Death. Continue along the walled path towards Swinbrook, looking out for the remains of an Italian terraced garden on the hillside, belonging to the wealthy Fettiplace family mansion, which was demolished in the early 19th century.

3. Upon reaching Swinbrook you pass St Mary's Church, which contains two spectacular wall tombs, each showing three Fettiplace gentlemen reclining on shelves – well worth a visit. One set was erected in 1613, the other, more elaborate set was carved by Oxford sculptor William Byrd in 1686. After passing through Swinbrook churchyard, follow the road round to the right. Pass the first footpath on the left, then take the next one on the left, opposite The Swan Inn. Or better still, nip into the inn for a little light refreshment!

4. Follow the footpath across the water meadows until you reach a junction, and take the right-hand fork towards the river. Continue on until you reach a bridge (but do not cross).

5. Cross the road by the bridge and rejoin the footpath, keeping the river to your right and passing Kitesbridge Farm to your left. After the farm, take the left-hand path uphill, away from the river. The path crosses the site of Akerman Street, a Roman road that ran between St Albans and Cirencester, passing through Asthall along the way.

6. At the top of the hill, turn right and walk for about 0.8km (½ mile) along the road, past the factory and car park, and over the bridge at Worsham. After crossing the bridge over the drain, turn right on to the bridleway back to Asthall and pass through three fields.

7. At the end of the third field, turn left along the hedge line, walking uphill, then turn right, following the path back to Asthall. Turn left at Asthall Farm, and then turn left again at the T-junction, which takes you back to The Maytime Inn.

8. You can extend this walk by parking in Burford and walking along the river to join the circular path at point 2 on the map. From Burford main car park cross the river bridge and turn left up Guildenford. Turn left into Witney Street and follow the road towards Widford. As you leave the houses of Burford behind, look out for a footpath in the meadow on the left. Follow this path next to the River Windrush until you meet up with the circular walk by Widford bridge.

Courtesy of Oxfordshire County Council. For similar walks see
www.oxfordshire.gov.uk/walksandrides or www.oxfordshirecotswolds.org/walks

THE COTSWOLD CLEARANCES

Widford is only one of about 80 deserted villages found scattered across the Cotswolds, many of which comprise little more than a series of bumps and hollows in the ground. The Black Death played its part in the desertions, but there were other factors, too. Cistercian monks, who were gifted land throughout the area in medieval times, would often move villagers from their expanding estates in order to maintain a life of solitude and meditation. In addition, the gradual decline of the feudal system, which saw farmers evicted from their land, and climate change, with severely cold winters and very hot summers causing crop failures and livestock disease, also contributed to the abandonment of villages.

In the Footsteps of a King

LEIGHTERTON AND WESTONBIRT ARBORETUM

This open level walk takes you over numerous stiles and across ancient fields surrounded by dry-stone walls to the edge of Westonbirt National Arboretum – one of the most spectacular tree collections in the world containing a staggering 18,000 catalogued trees (well worth a visit after your walk). From here you join up with the Monarch's Way which takes you back to Leighterton, where the walk finishes with a short tour of the village. Numerous meadow birds including the rare corn bunting can be seen along the way and hares are often sighted on the grassy slopes near the end of the walk.

DISTANCE:	8km (5 miles) (circular) or shorter route of 6.5km (4 miles)
TIME:	Allow 2½–3½ hours (shorter route: 2–2½ hours)
LEVEL:	Moderate, with many stiles
START/PARKING:	Park near The Royal Oak in Leighterton (GL8 8UN). OS grid reference ST823912 (OS Explorer map 168)
GETTING THERE:	*By car:* Take A46 Bath/Stroud road and take second of three turnings to Leighterton. Pass the school and turn right at the next junction *By public transport:* From Tetbury take bus no. 279 (limited service)
REFRESHMENTS:	The Royal Oak, Leighterton
LOCAL ATTRACTIONS:	Westonbirt National Arboretum; Police Museum at Tetbury Heritage Centre

DIRECTIONS

1. With your back to The Royal Oak main car-park entrance, turn right along the road and at the junction right again, to pass a red post box on the left. After 100m (110yd) turn left on to a footpath beyond a house called 'The Cuillins'. Cross three closely-spaced wooden stiles beside gates, then follow the path diagonally across several fields surrounded by dry-stone walls. Keep on course by checking back at each crossing to the previous stile, referring to the map. After a field adjacent to a group of barns, cross the stile and follow the wall on your left to the next stile. Now bear left to reach a drinking trough set in the stone wall opposite.

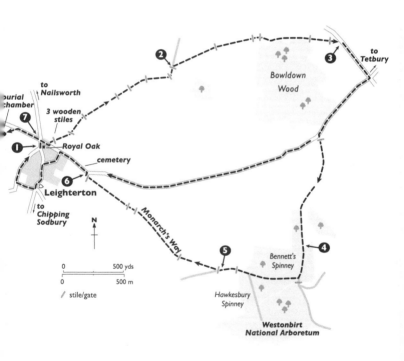

2. Cross the stile by the trough and climb half right to the top of the rise, where the next stile will be visible. Bear slightly right, but still go diagonally, to reach a gate near the far end of the right-hand wall. The trees of Bowldown Wood are a useful guide. (For the far-sighted, Tetbury spire in the distance makes a good marker.) Go through the gate and cut across the corner of the next field to another gate. Continue in the same direction near the edge of the wood. Go through another gate and then carry on in a similar direction to the road.

3. Turn right and walk along the wide verge to the crossroads in the dip. Turn right here and continue along the minor road until a right bend is reached just before an uphill section. Those who wish to take the shorter route can follow the road back to Leighterton via point 6 on the map (go straight to direction 6, below). The longer walk continues through the metal farm gate on the left. Follow the grassy track along the valley bottom with the field boundary on your right, and eventually pass through a farm gate into a wood.

4. This track (sometimes very muddy) ends in a clearing where the Monarch's Way meets it from the right. (The gate at this point leads you to a stile on the right into Westonbirt National Arboretum where you may choose to extend your walk – charges apply.) The walk now turns right along the Monarch's Way and passes westwards through the wood towards Leighterton. Don't be tempted along side tracks but keep going until you reach a farm gate. Pass through the gate and go straight ahead along a grassy route that passes between a wall on the left and some small ancient trees on the right. You will soon reach a wooden stile to the right of a metal gate.

5. Cross the stile and bear half right up the slope. At the top of the rise take care to aim for the jutting angle of the wall and continue to keep this wall on your right. Cross a stile. Further on, go over another stile near a farm gate and continue with the wall on your right to a stone stile in the wall. Cross and head gradually away from the wall towards a distant metal gate near the village that leads on to a lane. At the gate, go straight on along the lane into the village. Look out for the small cemetery on the right where you may find the time to spend a moment.

6. Continue along the lane and turn left at The Meads to take a short tour of the village (or, if you prefer, carry straight on to go back to your car). Pass a minute

chapel with a 'doll's house' porch and then the 13th-century church, which has an incongruous half-timbered tower: an economy measure when the Victorians ran out of cash and could not afford to replace the original castellated tower. Turn left at the next junction, passing the mellow Cotswold stone houses to reach the village duck pond with its noisy inhabitants. Go right at the crossroads (signed Bath Road) and then right at the T-junction. Pass Church Farm Barn (dating from 1733) which has been converted into a dwelling house but happily still retains its huge pigeon loft and dovecote. Continue back to your starting point at The Royal Oak.

7. At this point you can take a short detour by carrying on to the junction and turning left. Beyond the school on the left, some trees mark the site of the largest Neolithic burial chamber in the Cotswolds.

Courtesy of South Cotswold Ramblers. For more information go to www.southcotswoldramblers.org.uk

THE MONARCH'S WAY

The 2.5km (1½ miles) between Leighterton and Westonbirt Arboretum lies close to the route taken by King Charles II (of Scotland only at this stage) in 1651 as he fled across southern England, following his defeat by Cromwell's forces at the Battle of Worcester. Hotly pursued by Parliamentary troops and living off his wits, the 21-year-old King first headed north to Boscobel (where he famously hid in an oak tree) and then turned south, passing through the Cotswolds on his way to the coast, where he only narrowly avoided capture by embarking on a ship at Shoreham bound for France. Using footpaths and bridleways, the Monarch's Way is a 990km (615 miles) long-distance trail that closely follows Charles's erratic route, enabling walkers to visit the many historic sites along the way.

Golden Valley Walk

*This lovely walk links four Gloucestershire Wildlife Trust nature
reserves and showcases the natural beauty of the Golden Valley,
which was created by the melt-waters at the end of the last Ice Age.
A section of the route takes you along the old Thames and Severn
Canal, passing an old woollen mill along the way. The path then
climbs through Siccaridge Wood, a wonderful semi-natural ancient
woodland that has been coppiced for hundreds of years, where
bluebells and lily-of-the-valley bloom. Look out for ant hills
along the way, up to 50cm (20in) high and teeming with
wood ants in spring and summer.*

DISTANCE:	8km (5 miles) (circular)
TIME:	Allow 2½–3½ hours
LEVEL:	Moderate
START/PARKING:	The village of Daneway, 4.5km (3 miles) east of Stroud. Park in small lay-by or, for patrons, at the Daneway Inn car park (GL7 6LN). OS grid reference SO938034 (OS Explorer map 168)
GETTING THERE:	*By car:* From Stroud take the A419 and turn left towards Sapperton. At the next crossroads turn left past Sapperton village and down to the bottom of the hill *By public transport:* Contact Stroud Tourist Information
REFRESHMENTS:	The Daneway Inn or by car to The Crown in Frampton Mansell
LOCAL ATTRACTIONS:	The Alpaca Experience in the Cotswolds

DIRECTIONS

1. From the lay-by walk across the old canal bridge and turn left into Hillhouse Lane, which takes you past Siccaridge Wood Nature Reserve. Continue over the brow of the hill and down to the bottom where a field gate can be seen on the left. Do not go through the gate into the reserve at this point; instead, carry along the drive until you reach a public footpath on the left.

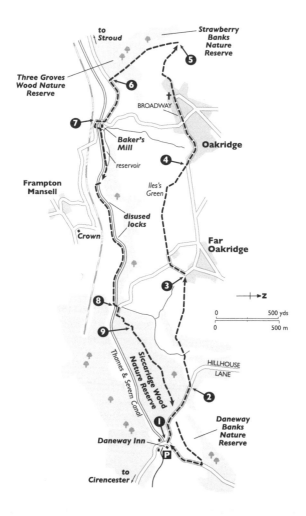

2. Turn down the footpath and after approximately 100m (110yd) go through a gate and into a small field. Cross the stile and bridge into the next field. The path now starts to climb the valley and into an area of ancient woodland known as Peyton's Grove. The footpath continues through the wood and into pastureland. Follow the path across two fields in the direction of the farm at the top of the slope.

3. When you reach the road on the edge of Far Oakridge, turn left and follow the small lane until it runs sharply to the right. At this point go through the stile into the field. This stretch of the walk is called Iles's Green. After a short walk through the field, cross the stile and follow the path up to the top corner of the field. Go over the stile and keep to the left-hand field boundary until the next stile is reached on the edge of Oakridge village. In spring and summer the banks at the top of these two fields are full of pretty wild flowers such as primroses, cowslips and celandines.

4. Turn left on to the road known as the Broadway and continue to the village green. Walk along the bottom of the green past the church (built in 1837) on your left. Pass between the cottages and over a stile that leads out of the village and into a small field. Follow the path down to the left until another stile is reached. A spring is close to the path at this point and the area can be quite wet. Once across the stile turn right and follow the path diagonally down to the corner of the field to Strawberry Banks Nature Reserve.

5. Enter the reserve via the gate and into a linear section of scrub that forms the fringe of the northern boundary. Go right and walk down the path until the scrub tunnel opens up on to the main part of the reserve. At the bottom of the slope the path meets with another path. Turn left and follow the contour of the valley until you reach Three Groves Wood Nature Reserve, but avoid dropping down to the stream. Once in the wood follow the path down the side of the valley until you reach a small lane.

6. Turn left on to the lane and you will see Baker's Mill in the distance. Halfway to the mill is a spring known locally as Ashmeads Spring. This was one of the springs that used to provide water for the residents of Oakridge. Continue until the road forks and Baker's Mill is now in front of you.

Of Mice and Other Mammals

Siccaridge Wood Nature Reserve is home to the common dormouse, now protected under European law. Hibernating from September to April, these tiny mammals spend the summer months in the dense shrub layer, feeding mainly on flowers, pollen, fruits and insects. They build their nests in tree-holes or special dormouse boxes, which allow licensed handlers to monitor their numbers (please do not look inside the boxes). Other small mammals you may hear but probably not see include the wood mouse and the yellow-necked mouse. Signs of fallow deer, roe deer and hedgehogs can also be seen along the paths.

7. From here the walk follows the route of the old Thames and Severn Canal. Take the right turn at Baker's Mill and cross the old canal bridge. From the bridge you can see the footbridge that leads from the road to the towpath. Once on the towpath turn right. The first part of the walk passes Baker's Mill Reservoir, which would have powered the mill. Continue along the towpath, passing a disused lock on your right and cross over the canal bridge. Turn immediately left so that the lock is now on your left and follow the footpath sign that takes you along the towpath to Whitehall Bridge.

8. Cross over the bridge into Siccaridge Nature Reserve. Follow the public footpath up into the wood for a few metres and then take the right-hand path, carrying on up the slope until it levels out slightly at an open glade where four footpaths meet.

9. Take the path on the right that leads uphill. After a short walk you will reach another open glade. Continue on the path down the slope until you reach the field gate at the reserve boundary that you passed earlier. Opposite is the entrance into Daneway Banks Nature Reserve. At this point you can either turn right and retrace your steps to your starting point or extend your walk by looping through the reserve, as shown on the map.

Courtesy of Gloucestershire Wildlife Trust. For more information about the wildlife on this walk go to www.gloucestershirewildlifetrust.co.uk/reserves

North Face of the Cotswolds

ILMINGTON

This panoramic walk on pasture and farm tracks starts in Ilmington, a North Cotswolds village that lies nestled beneath Ilmington Downs, the highest point in Warwickshire. After visiting the historic village church and seeking out its 11 carved mice and embroidered apple map, you climb 140m (460ft) through a country estate to the top of the downs, encountering sheep, pheasants and perhaps the occasional buzzard along the way. The climb is well worth the effort as the summit provides spectacular views to the north, south, east and west as far away as Wales. The return journey has the added bonus of passing the site of an English Civil War battle.

DISTANCE:	8km (5 miles) (circular)
TIME:	Allow 2½–3½ hours
LEVEL:	Moderate, after a climb of 140m (460ft)
START/PARKING:	St Mary's Church, Back Street, Ilmington (CV36 4LJ). OS grid reference SP208434 (OS Explorer map 205). Park in Back Street near the church
GETTING THERE:	*By car:* Take A44 from Oxford, then A429 from Moreton-in-Marsh, turning left to Ilmington as signposted, shortly after junction with B4035
	By public transport: Train to Stratford-upon-Avon, then bus no. 23/23A to Ilmington (not Sundays)
REFRESHMENTS:	The Red Lion or The Howard Arms, Ilmington
LOCAL ATTRACTIONS:	Hidcote Manor Garden (National Trust); Court Barn (Arts and Crafts) Museum, Chipping Campden

DIRECTIONS

1. Start your walk in the fine Norman church of St Mary's. Hidden around the church you will find 11 carved mice, the signature of master carpenter Robert Thompson of Kilburn. On the wall is an embroidered apple map, celebrating Ilmington's orchard heritage. From the church door take the short path to the graveyard gate and turn left by a wooden lamp post. At the second lamp post bear right with a thatched cottage on your left. Pass a damson orchard, cross the road ahead, and climb half-right on a grassy path towards the war memorial. Turn right and follow the road ahead into Grump Street.

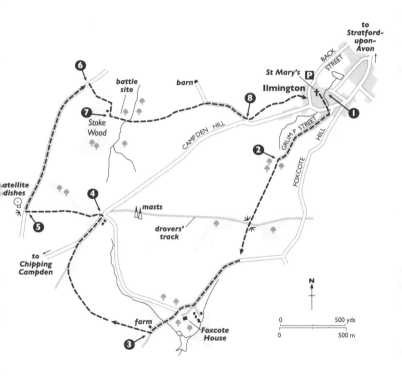

2. Where the road ends keep straight on under the trees as far as a wide gate ahead. Before the gate turn right downhill on a narrow path with yellow arrows and go through two kissing gates into a meadow. Here turn left and climb steadily for 15 minutes alongside the line of willows until you cross an old drover's track, with great views behind you and ahead towards a distant mansion. Take the track ahead downhill to join a metalled drive, then turn right towards Foxcote House. At the house turn right on the drive, go downhill and then up past a farmhouse to a gate on your right.

3. From the gate, take the grassy path uphill to a wooden gate and carry on (this stretch may be churned up by horses) to the top where you turn right on a wide track among new woodland to a road. Here turn right and walk on the right-hand side past a bungalow and an entrance gate to Foxcote. Just before a track goes uphill on the right, cross the road with care and go through a small wooden gate into a paddock with an oak tree in the middle; this is a good sheltered spot to pause. (If there are any horses here, continue on to the field above.)

4. From the tree climb through a metal gate under the trees and carry on up to a level path between a hedge and a dry-stone wall. Approaching a cluster of masts and satellite dishes ahead you have reached your summit of the day – 261m (856ft) – with huge views across the Severn Vale to the Malverns and, on a clear day, to the Black Mountains in Wales.

5. Turn right down the lane. Unless someone has removed them you'll pass 21 limestone rocks – this soft, porous stone is what the Cotswolds are made of. Millions of years ago it was warm seaside around here, so see if you can find any tiny fossils or seashells in the rocks. The lane gets steeper as you walk further down.

6. Opposite a double metal gate on the left, find an inconspicuous wooden bridleway post at the end of the hedge on your right. Turn right across the ploughed field to a new plantation, and fork left among the young trees, following the yellow arrows down to a private drive leading to a house on your right. Go through both gates and turn right in the field alongside the drive, without losing height.

7. Opposite the house a small promontory is the site of a fortress built by the Cavaliers in the English Civil War. The Roundheads stormed it one dark night and after a short battle took the King's men off to Warwick until their families paid the ransom to get them back. Still close to the house fence, go through a five-barred gate and turn left downhill on rough pasture (with the hedge on your left) towards a stream. The last bit can be slippery. Cross the culvert bridge and bear left uphill to a narrow wooden bridge. Cross it and climb the grassy slope ahead, keeping to the right of a lone tree at the top. Go ahead through a wide gate and follow the easy track that curves along the hillside for five minutes.

8. Just before the track meets up with a lane turn left through a wide gate and stile. Round the corner take the raised grassy track (an old road) downhill towards the church where you started. As you enter the village go through the wide gate ahead into a sunken lane, and you will find yourself back at St Mary's Church.

Courtesy of Stephen Wright, Voluntary Warden, Cotswolds Conservation Board. For more information go to www.cotswoldsaonb.org.uk

THE MOUSEMAN OF KILBURN

Born in 1876 in Kilburn, North Yorkshire, Robert Thompson is widely regarded as one of the country's finest craftsmen of traditional oak furniture. Although he never left the cottage in which he was born, so great was his reputation in the early 20th century that he was widely commissioned by architects to create work for cathedrals, churches and stately homes across Britain and abroad. His signature carved mouse adorns every piece he ever made, including those to be found in St Mary's, Ilmington. The origin of the mouse is uncertain, but once story goes that he carved his first one in response to one of his craftsmen commenting: 'We are as poor as church mice!'

Ancient Woodland Walk

LOWER WOODS NATURE RESERVE

Combining three waymarked routes, clearly colour-coded on rough oak posts, this glorious walk takes you through a medieval landscape of ancient woods and coppices, surrounded by ancient woodbanks and separated by old grassy roads, or 'trenches'. Lower Woods is one of the largest oak-ash woods in the country and is nationally important for its woodland flowers. In addition, bats, stoats, dormice, roe deer, badgers, foxes, breeding songbirds and over-wintering woodcock, along with many butterfly, beetle, moth, hoverfly and dragonfly species combine to make it a paradise of wildlife.

DISTANCE:	7km (4½ miles) (circular) or a shorter route of 4.5km (3 miles)
TIME:	2–3 hours (shorter route: 1½–2 hours)
LEVEL:	Moderate, with one steep climb
START/PARKING:	Lower Woods Lodge, about 1.5km (1 mile) east of Wickwar (GL9 1BY); parking on site. OS grid reference ST746882 (OS Explorer map 167)
GETTING THERE:	*By car:* Turn off M4 at junction 18 on to A46 northbound; after 9.5km (6 miles) turn left to Hawkesbury Upton. Go through village then turn left to Wickwar at the Hawkesbury Monument. Cross cattle grid and common, then turn left to Lower Woods opposite sign to Inglestone Farm *By public transport:* Train to Yate, then bus no. 84 to Wickwar (not Sundays)
REFRESHMENTS:	The Beaufort Inn, Hawkesbury Upton
LOCAL ATTRACTIONS:	Horton Court (National Trust)

DIRECTIONS

1. Start the walk at gate 1, beside the 17th century Lodge (once the site of a Roman villa), and follow the red waymarked Stanley Walk into the Stanley Meadow (waymark 2) and on into Stanley Orchard (3). The small hunting gate (4) is a reminder that hunting has taken place in Lower Woods from early times.

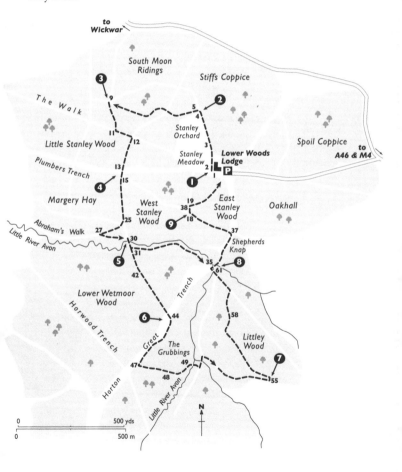

2. The path now turns left along a woodland ride, bordering Stiffs Coppice (waymark 5). In this typical hazel coppice, where each coppiced tree has many stems, bluebells are abundant in spring, and diverse wildlife, from insects to dormice, feeds on the hazel. Notice how the coppice contains many oaks that escaped felling and are now over 100 years old.

3. Bear sharp left at waymark 9 and turn left on to The Walk at 11. This fashionably straight walk was created in the 1690s and was designed to give a clear view from the Lodge (which originally had a rooftop viewing platform) all the way to Wickwar Church. Turn right at 12 and pass through Little Stanley Wood, coppiced in the 1990s, then cross over the ancient Plumbers Trench at 13, a wide and sunny path with large banks and many wet patches, ideal for butterflies and grassland plants.

4. Leave the red route at waymark 15 and keep following the green waymarked Little Avon Circuit, turning into Margery Hay at 25 to avoid the mud and to see the delicate pink flowers of the autumn crocus (meadow saffron) blooming in September. The path takes a sharp left at 27, bringing you into Abraham's Walk, comprising long, damp riverside meadows that are rich in wild flowers such as water avens and false oxlip.

5. Cross the bridge over the Little Avon River at waymark 30. Now you can either extend your walk by taking the yellow waymarked Littley Loop (31) or turn left and follow the green route along the riverside to 35 – a beautiful walk shaded by oak, ash and alders, where wood anemone and bluebell clothe the woodland slope in spring (go straight to direction 8, below, to complete this shorter route). To continue along the yellow route, enter a tall, dense oakwood where the trees were last felled around 1850. As a result the wood is becoming high forest, where many trees continue to grow while others die, which is good for fungi, woodpeckers and deadwood insects. Look out for two varieties of pendunculate (English) oak opposite waymark 42: the one uneven, brownish and bristly, and native to Lower Woods, the other straight and grey-barked, an alien variety planted in the 18th–19th centuries for its high-quality timber.

6. Turn right at waymark 44 along the Horton Great Trench, probably pre-Roman in origin and once the main route from Wotton-Under-Edge to Bristol. It is now home to 20 species of butterfly, including the white admiral and silver-washed fritillary, and a host of wild flowers, such as cornflower blue and devil's bit scabious. Then turn into the The Grubbings at 47, an area 'grubbed out' in the 1890s to create a grassy vista, but reverted to woodland after 1947 with silver birch, hawthorn, aspen and oak. Look out for deserted anthills between 48 and 49, survivals from the open grassland days.

7. After a sharp U-turn at waymark 55 the path takes you through Littley Wood. There is some mystery about this wood, as adder's tongue – a fern more often seen in ancient grasslands – is widespread and there are hornbeams 6m (20ft) before 58, which are uncommon in ancient woodlands in this area. At 61 you emerge on to common land at a spot once called Kilvers Pill.

8. Rejoining the green route at waymark 35, cross over the bridge and climb the steep slope up Shepherds Knap to East Stanley Wood. At 18/38, where the green route briefly merges with the red route, an area on your left called the 'island' is rich in wild flowers, including herb paris and autumn crocus.

9. Fork right at waymark 19 and follow the red route back to your starting point.

Courtesy of Gloucestershire Wildlife Trust. For more information on this and similar walks go to www.gloucestershirewildlifetrust.co.uk/reserves

ANCIENT COPPICING

From early times these woods were managed as coppice-with-standards, a system that provided a wonderful habitat for wildlife that still survives today. Mature oak standards were grown for timber, while hazel, field maple and ash were coppiced, that is, cut to ground level on an 18-year cycle to encourage the growth of multiple stems that could be used for charcoal, firewood and fencing, among other things. The large ancient woodbanks that are a feature of Lower Woods were built to protect the coppices from grazing animals during the first nine years of regrowth. Today they are rich in wild flowers and are criss-crossed by deer and badger tracks.

Cranham, Cooper's and the Beechwoods

*This beautiful walk takes you along a section of the
Cotswold Way, through one of England's most treasured
habitats – ancient beech woodlands – and on to the site of possibly
the Cotswold's most intriguing tradition: cheese-rolling. En route
you will discover the cathedral-like calm of Buckholt Wood, part
of a national nature reserve that is richly carpeted with bluebells
in May, and the dizzy heights of Cooper's Hill, with its fine
panoramic views. It is from the top of this hill, possibly
for hundreds of years, that the foolhardy have risked
their necks for cheese and glory!*

DISTANCE:	6.5km (4 miles) (circular)
TIME:	Allow 2–3½ hours
LEVEL:	Easy
START/PARKING:	In the car park on the western outskirts of Cranham village (GL4 8HP). OS grid reference SO893131 (OS Explorer sheet 179)
GETTING THERE:	*By car:* Exit M5 at junction 11A on to A417 towards Cirencester; turn off on to A46 towards Brockworth and continue along winding road until left-hand turnoff for Cranham (park before reaching village centre) *By public transport:* By train to Cheltenham Spa or Stroud, then bus no. 46 to Cranham Corner, with 0.8km (½ mile) walk to starting point
REFRESHMENTS:	The Black Horse, Cranham
LOCAL ATTRACTIONS:	Great Witcombe Roman Villa (English Heritage); Prinknash Bird and Deer Park

DIRECTIONS

1. Starting out under the ancient beech tree in the little car park, enter into the majestic Buckholt Wood and take the middle of the three clear paths ahead of you. This wood forms part of the Cotswold Commons and Beechwoods National Nature Reserve, an internationally important site, containing as it does some of Britain's finest beechwoods. Continue up the path for just under 0.8km (½ mile) until you reach the small car park next to the road. Keeping a good look out for traffic, cross straight over and continue to follow the path through the woods on the other side.

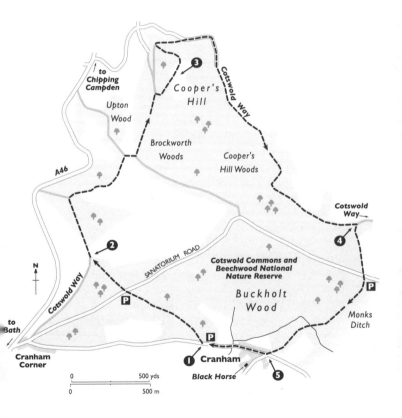

2. At the top of the hill, veer right to follow the Cotswold Way as it comes in from the left and follow the signs for just over 0.8km (½ mile). At the top, turn right and pass through the kissing gate with pasture on either side and continue to follow the Cotswold Way off to the left. Stay on the trail as it snakes up through the woods until you emerge out into the open at the top of Cooper's Hill, a local nature reserve in which the beechwoods and flower-rich limestone grasslands are of national importance.

3. For generations Cooper's Hill has been home to the annual cheese-rolling festival. The origins of this intriguing tradition are lost in the mists of time, but there are records of the event dating back to the 1800s when it was part of a larger event called a 'wake'. Nowadays, thousands of spectators flock from all over the world on the spring bank holiday to watch people hurl themselves down the hill after a speeding 3kg (7lb) Double Gloucester. Gazing down this vertiginous slope, it is hard to believe that anyone ever walks away – some don't! To start the second half of your walk, follow the Cotswold Way steeply downhill to your left and back into the woods, turning right and emerging out through a kissing gate at the bottom of the hill. Continue on to the road, turning right to head along past the last few houses. At the end of the road, pass through a gate on to a track.

4. After following this track along the edge and through the woods for 1.5km (1 mile), you reach a marker post and a field gate on your left with a view down to the lakes in the distance. Leaving the Cotswold Way behind, take the path up to the right and back into Buckholt Wood. After a short while, emerge out on to a drive and head right up towards the road. Keeping a good lookout, cross the road and take the path directly

WILDLIFE WATCH

These wildlife-rich woodlands support an outstanding flora, with carpets of bluebells and wood anemone widespread in spring, plus many rare species such as stinking hellebore, bird's nest orchid, yellow bird's nest, wood barley and white helleborine. Invertebrates include rare spiders and Britain's largest snail, the rare Roman snail, plus a range of butterflies including the silver-washed fritillary and, less commonly, the white admiral and white-letter hairstreak. Birds such as the tawny owl, buzzard, great spotted woodpecker, nuthatch, treecreeper and wood warbler are also to be found, along with flocks of finches (including brambling) feeding on the beech mast in the winter. The flower-rich grasslands that surround the woods contain cowslip, frog orchid, kidney vetch and autumn gentian, providing colour through spring and summer, and food plants support small blue, chalkhill blue, brown argus and small heath butterflies. The rough grassland is also ideal for lizards, adders and grass snakes.

opposite. As you reach the small car parking area under the trees, make for the track at the far side, and head downhill past the large house. Continue down the track and straight on to a footpath with a crumbled old stone wall on your left, eventually passing over a trickling stream next to another ancient beech tree. Carry on up through the woods until you emerge out into open common land, and follow the track past the houses on the right until you meet the road opposite the little bus stop.

5. Take the road down through Cranham and, should you have a thirst in need of quenching after your walk, turn left opposite the next footpath sign up towards the inviting Black Horse Inn. After this most pleasing of detours, continue to follow the road down through the village and back up towards the car park at the start.

Courtesy of the Natural England/Cotswold Way National Trail. For updated information on this walk and for similar walks see www.nationaltrail.co.uk/Cotswold

Cotswold Canal Walk

BRIMSCOMBE AND CHALFORD

*This fascinating walk leads you through the Cotswolds'
industrial past, following a section of the Thames and Severn
Canal as it slowly climbs the Frome valley towards the summit at
Daneway, 95m (310ft) above sea level. Along the way you pass a
series of locks – some recently restored, others derelict, a few infilled
– plus a beautifully restored round house, several old woollen mills
given a new lease of life as offices, and a towering Victorian
railway viaduct. Although the canal was abandoned
in 1933, an ongoing restoration programme is slowly
returning it to its former glory, with the help of the
Cotswold Canals Trust.*

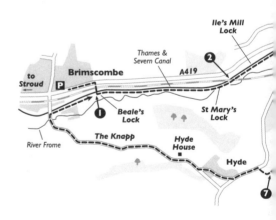

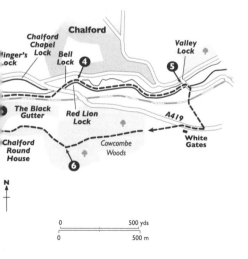

DIRECTIONS

1. From the lay-by cross the turnpike road and walk along to the railway crossing (opposite the restaurant) where, not so long ago, Brimscombe Station once stood with its locomotive sheds housing banker or 'pusher' engines that helped with the long climb up the Sapperton incline. You are now at Beale's Lock. Cross the bridge over the tail of the lock and turn left towards Chalford. The water in the pound (the chamber between the lock gates) was once used to top up the water tanks of steam locomotives. Walk 0.8km (½ mile) to St Mary's Lock along one of the most attractive sections of the valley.

2. Carry on alongside the canal as it continues to climb. You soon reach Ile's Mill Lock and further on you will come to a row of garages on the site of Ballinger's Lock, with Chalford Round House visible ahead of you. This was one of five distinctive round houses built along the canal in the 1780s, designed to house the lengthmen who were responsible for stretches of the canal. The canal is infilled for a short distance past the former Smart's coal yard (look out for the advert painted on the wall), as is Chapel Lock further along, just after where the towpath crosses the road. As you pass the Round House, note the mile plate above the entrance to the culvert.

3. Leave the canal as it makes its way in much narrower form behind the factory building, and turn right down the road opposite the church. The road swings to the right but go straight on down the footpath to the edge of the railway line. Follow the path to the left and soon you will hear the rushing water of copious springs known locally as 'The Black Gutter', which once supplied water to the canal. It is now hidden away by the water authority. Follow the path between the railway line and the former Bliss Mills complex to bring you back to the canal. Now cross the A419 with care, and continue along the towpath, with the canal now on your right, past the head of Bell Lock and on to Red Lion Lock.

4. The canal continues on its way, squeezed against the valley side by the now shrunken millpond of Seville's Mill. Towering above the canal is the railway line, precariously perched on a half viaduct. The canal now widens on the approach to Valley Lock. The building on the far side of the bridge was once known variously as The Valley Inn and The Clothiers Arms. Cross the bridge

and fork right up the hillside immediately past this former hostelry.

5. Before crossing the railway line stop and enjoy the view down into the valley, then continue up the hillside, with the fence line on your left, through the woods until you reach the A419 once more. Turn right and walk down the road for a short way, then cross on to the tarmac drive at White Gates. Follow the footpath up across the field with its humps and dips into Cowcombe Woods.

6. Your path now follows a (more or less) level route along the hillside, with fields eventually appearing on the right. After a short while the path becomes a track with a view down the valley towards Burleigh and Swellshill and, to the right, Skaites Hill House. Civilisation returns with the settlement of Hyde.

7. Join Hyde Hill for a short walk up the hill before rejoining the lane past Hyde End House. Follow the lane through National Trust land, past Hyde House and along to The Knapp. Here you have a panoramic view down over the start of your walk. The lane now becomes quite steep as it drops down the hillside towards the sites of Wimberley and Dark Mills. Turn right along the towpath, with the canal on your left, and follow the path until you reach Beale's Lock once more, then cross over the canal and railway line to reach your starting point.

Courtesy of the Cotswold Canals Trust. For more information visit www.cotswoldcanals.com

THE THAMES AND SEVERN CANAL

Completed in 1789, the Thames and Severn Canal was designed to link these two great rivers and provide transport for the many woollen mills that lined the deep valley, powered by the rushing waters of the River Frome. Thames barges could reach as far as Wallbridge in Stroud, where the canal joined up with the wider Stroudwater Canal (1775–79), enabling large sea-going Severn trows (a type of cargo boat) to take over the burden. The canal proved highly profitable, reaching its peak in 1841, but with the coming of the railways business started to decline, and by 1893 the section east of Chalford was closed. Subsequent attempts to revitalize it proved unsuccessful and by 1933 the entire length of the canal was abandoned.

Mills and Meadows Walk

STOW-ON-THE-WOLD
TO BOURTON-ON-THE-WATER

*This easy downhill walk from Stow-on-the-Wold to
Bourton-on-the-Water, passing mills and meadows along the
way, is specially designed for those wanting to leave the car at
home. Stow-on-the-Wold is one of the Cotswolds' loveliest towns,
little changed since the days when The Square thronged with sheep
rather than cars. The route then leads you through the picturesque
village of Lower Slaughter where the old flour mill has recently
been restored and now houses a teashop, small store and museum.
A short detour takes you upstream to the equally pretty village
of Upper Slaughter, criss-crossing the River Eye over
quaint old bridges along the way.*

DISTANCE:	6.5km (4 miles) with 1.5km (1 mile) extension
TIME:	Allow 2–2½ hours (2½–3 hours with extension)
LEVEL:	Easy
START/PARKING:	St Edward's Hall, Stow Square in Stow-on-the-Wold (GL54 1AF). Park in Bourton-on-the-Water and take bus no. 801 or 855 (not Sundays) to starting point. OS grid reference SP191257 (OS Explorer sheet OL45)
GETTING THERE:	*By car:* Take A40 from Oxford then head north on A429, turning right just after junction with A436. *By public transport:* By train to Moreton-in-Marsh, then bus no. 801 or 855. Bus returns to station from Bourton High Street
REFRESHMENTS:	The Mousetrap Inn, Bourton-on-the-Water or The Old Mill teashop in Lower Slaughter
LOCAL ATTRACTIONS:	Birdland Park and Gardens; Cotswold Motoring Museum and Toy Collection

DIRECTIONS

1. Starting from St Edward's Hall leave the south end of Stow Square via Church Street, walking along past the church until you reach Sheep Street. Cross at the traffic lights and walk along Wragg's Row, crossing Back Walls at the end of the row and entering the burial ground. Leave the cemetery by the second gate on your right and walk down South Hill, which follows the route of the Fosse Way Roman Road. When you are about 150m (165yd) beyond Bretton House cross the Fosse Way to a track with a footpath sign, next to Quarwood Cottage.

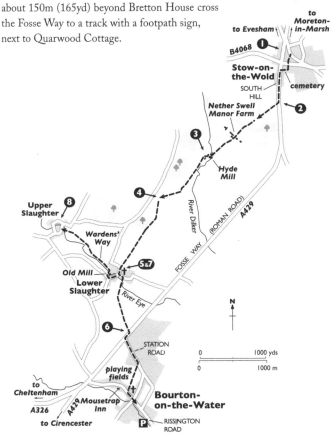

2. Follow the track to a field. Cross the field into woodland and continue down through Nether Swell Manor Farm and the paddock beyond to reach Hyde Mill. As you cross the meadows, look out for kestrels hovering overhead, and the occasional kingfisher as you approach the River Dilker. Here, banded demoiselle and large red damselflies skim the surface, and brown trout, bullhead and brook lamprey lurk in the crystal-clear water.

3. Cross the bridge and walk round the farm buildings. Turn right at the signpost to Lower Slaughter, then turn left through the metal kissing gate to a small bridge. Follow the path across four fields, then cross a stream and turn right through a gate. Cross the field to the gate in the far-left corner.

4. Turn half left to follow the sign to Lower Slaughter and cross three more fields, turning right through a farm gate just before the end of the third field. Now turn left to follow the hedge line, past the cricket ground, then turn right to join the road into Lower Slaughter. Turn left, keeping the church wall on your left, and follow the road round to the churchyard.

5. At this point you can extend your walk by taking a detour to the twin village of Upper Slaughter, a mere 0.8km (½ mile) to the north west following the River Eye (see directions 7 and 8). Otherwise, cross the road and turn left to follow the River Eye southwards on the path around to the right. Continue along to a metal gate leading to The Coach and Horses, a 400-year-old coaching house on the Fosse Way.

6. Cross the road with care and turn right. When you reach the T-junction turn left down Station Road towards Bourton. About 50m (55yd) past Meadow Way on your left, cross the road and take the path alongside the playing fields. Pass the church on your left to reach Bourton-on-the-Water High Street. Regularly voted one of England's prettiest villages, Bourton has more than its fair share of honey-coloured cottages, some of which date back to Elizabethan times. If you travelled by train, the Pulham 801 or 855 bus will take you back to Moreton-in-Marsh.

UPPER AND LOWER SLAUGHTERS

These quaint Cotswold villages, set only a short walk apart, are not as sinister as their names might suggest. The term 'slaughter' in fact stems from the Old English words 'slough' or 'slothre', meaning a wetland or muddy place, a reference to the damp land surrounding the little Eye stream (also known as the Slaughter Brook) upon which both villages lie. Today the Slaughters are far from muddy and, with no building work having taken place here since 1906, they have changed little in the last century, thus epitomizing the idyllic Cotswold village. Of particular note is St Peter's in Upper Slaughter, a historic Norman church with parts dating back to the 12th century and with a 15th-century tower.

7. For the detour to Upper Slaughter, follow the road round to the right until you reach the Old Mill, built in the 19th century and featuring a giant working water wheel. Now a museum with a tea and gift shop, it makes an ideal place to stop for refreshments. Take the footpath that runs along the side of the mill, signposted 'Wardens' Way', walking along the riverbank and crossing three fields. Listen and look out for water voles as you follow the river's course. Cross a stone footbridge over the river and carry on to the road, then turn right. Re-cross the river and turn immediately left where it is sign posted 'unsuitable for motors'. Continue for 150m (165yd) then, at the ford, re-cross the river by a stone footbridge.

8. Walk up the hill until you reach the small village square, where the cottages were reconstructed by famous Edwardian architect Edward Lutyens. Once you've explored the village, retrace your steps back to Lower Slaughter and follow direction 5.

Courtesy of the Cotswolds Conservation Board.
For more information see cotswoldsaonb.org.uk

Broadway Tower Walk

*Starting off in the quintessential English village of
Broadway, located in the northern tip of the Cotswolds on the
Worcestershire/Gloucestershire border, this enchanting walk leads
you along historic tracks, through kissing gates and across fields to
the top of Broadway Hill which, at a height of 312m (1,024ft),
is the second-highest point in the Cotswolds. Here you can follow
in the footsteps of William Morris and visit Broadway Tower,
an intriguing 18th-century folly from where on a clear day
you can see 13 counties. The route then joins up with
the Cotswold Way to take you back to your
starting point.*

DISTANCE: 6.5km (4 miles) (circular)

TIME: Allow 2–2½ hours

LEVEL: Moderate, with some steep sections and stiles

START/PARKING: The High Street, Broadway (WR12 7AA), with parking at Church Close, off Church Street. OS grid reference SP096375 (OS Explorer map OL45)

GETTING THERE: *By car:* Turning off A44 Oxford/ Worcester Road
By public transport: Bus no. 606 from Cheltenham (not Sundays)

REFRESHMENTS: The Crown and Trumpet Inn, Broadway; also Rookery Barn café at Broadway Tower Country Park

LOCAL ATTRACTIONS: Snowshill Manor; Stanway Water Garden

DIRECTIONS

1. Often referred to as 'the Jewel of the Cotswolds', with its origins possibly dating back to Roman times, Broadway became a magnet for artists in the late 19th century, following its discovery by William Morris and his artist friends. Famous visitors included JM Barrie, Vaughan Williams, Edward Elgar and John Singer Sargent, and leading furniture-designer Gordon Russell set

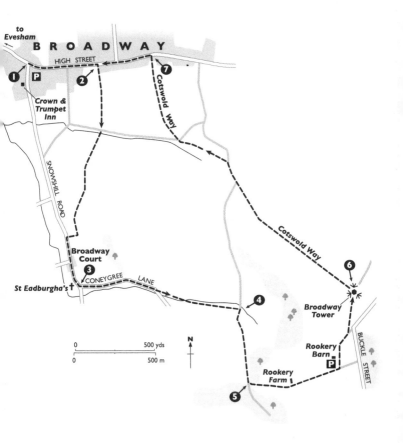

up his workshop here in 1927. Start at the war memorial at the bottom of the grass-fringed High Street and walk eastwards up past the red phone boxes. Continue on past the shops until you reach a sign pointing right towards the activity park and picnic area.

2. Follow this path between the avenue of trees with the playground on your left, and pass through the kissing gate at the end. Continue straight across the field, through the kissing gate at the other side, over a small footbridge and through another gate into a 'ridge and furrow' field. Be wary of muddy areas near these gates after wet weather. Continue to follow the direction arrows through two more kissing gates and fields until you reach the road. Watching for traffic, turn left and continue up Snowshill Road until you reach St Eadburgha's Church, parts of which date back to the 11th century.

3. Turn left just after the church through the gateway into Coneygree Lane, named after the medieval 'free' rabbit (or coney) warren granted here by Henry III in 1251, which was a form of hunting license. Follow the track uphill for just over 0.8km (½ mile).

4. At the top of the track, turn right and continue on through a two-in-one gate, following the path through the field to the house at the top. Follow the track to the right of the house until you reach two field gates.

5. On reaching a farm gate with two stone gateposts turn left through the gate and up the track until you reach Rookery Farm. Keeping the farm buildings on your left, continue straight on up the metalled track until you see a kissing gate on the left. Go through the gate into the grounds of the Rookery Barn café. Just by the main entrance pass through the tall kissing gate and head on up towards the tower.

6. You are now at the second highest point in the Cotswolds with its beautiful landscape laid out beneath you, so take a few minutes to soak in the breathtaking views over fields, hills and hedgerows as far as South Wales in the distance. A climb up the tower, built for Lady Coventry in 1798, is well worth the small fee, providing as it does one of England's outstanding viewpoints (see special feature, below). To continue the walk, pass through a second high kissing gate beyond the tower on to the Cotswold Way and turn left down towards a stile. Follow the Cotswold Way signs down the hill for 1.5km (1 mile), keeping the wonderful dry-stone wall on your right, and

passing over several stone stiles and down one flight of steps. Towards the bottom, the path levels out; continue to follow the signs through two metal kissing gates and over a stream, heading for the houses at the far side of the last field. Pass through two more gates and follow the alley towards the road.

7. Turn left and continue down the High Street, back towards the memorial at your starting point. The Crown and Trumpet Inn on Church Street is the perfect place to rest tired feet and to plan your next walk.

Courtesy of the Natural England/Cotswold Way National Trail. For updated information on this walk and for similar walks see www.nationaltrail.co.uk/Cotswold

A HEADY RETREAT

Designed by leading Georgian architect James Wyatt to resemble a mock Saxon castle, and built atop a 'beacon' hill (where beacons were lit in Elizabethan times to warn of the approaching Spanish Armada), Broadway Tower stands 17m (55ft) tall, providing spectacular views across the Vales of Evesham and Gloucester, and as far as the Severn Valley and the Welsh mountains beyond. Designer, writer and craftsman William Morris holidayed here with his family in 1876, in search of a quiet retreat for his ailing daughter who had recently been diagnosed with epilepsy. Fixated as he was with towers, he found the building both mad and marvelous, 'among the winds and the clouds'. If you visit the tower you will find the Morris Room furnished with some of his more famous designs.

String of Pearls Walk

NAILSWORTH, PINFARTHINGS AND BOX

*Routed along minor country roads and well-worn common
and woodland paths, this fascinating walk explores the area's
once-thriving woollen industry, which dates back hundreds of
years. Of the 150 mills that once scattered the steep valleys
surrounding Stroud – poetically known as the 'string of pearls' –
twelve were built in and around Nailsworth, of which four can
be viewed en route. There is only one very steep section that climbs
from the valley floor by Dunkirk Mills towards Minchinhampton
Common, where the superb limestone grasslands support orchids,
such as autumn lady's-tresses, and a variety of butterflies,
including the small blue, chalkhill blue, brown argus
and small heath.*

DISTANCE:	5.5km (3½ miles) (circular)
TIME:	Allow 1½–2 hours
LEVEL:	Moderate, with one very steep section
START/PARKING:	Car park on Newmarket Road, Nailsworth (nearby postcode: GL6 0DG) OS grid reference ST847994 (OS Explorer map 168)
GETTING THERE:	*By car:* South of Stroud, on A46
	By public transport: Train to Stroud, then no. 46 Stroud/Forest Green bus to Nailsworth
REFRESHMENTS:	The Britannia and The Jovial Forester, Nailsworth
LOCAL ATTRACTIONS:	All Saints Church, Selsley (Arts and Crafts gem with stained glass by William Morris, Edward Burne-Jones, William Rossetti et al)

DIRECTIONS

1. From Nailsworth car park turn left along Newmarket Road until you reach Christ Church on your right. On your left you will see Prices Mill Surgery, previously a paper mill, a corn mill, a brass foundry and an undertakers, until it was refurbished in 1996 as a health centre. Cross the road and climb the steep footpath with the handrail at the far end of the church wall. At the top turn right along the road, called The Rollers. Ignoring Chestnut Hill on your right, continue up Fewster Road, passing a small garage on the left before reaching Spring Hill coming up from the right. Cross over and continue along Northfields Road, enjoying, along the way, the fine views of Watledge across the valley. Further along the village of Amberley comes into view, perched on the hillside, and you get your first sight of Dunkirk Mills in the valley below (see special feature, page 83).

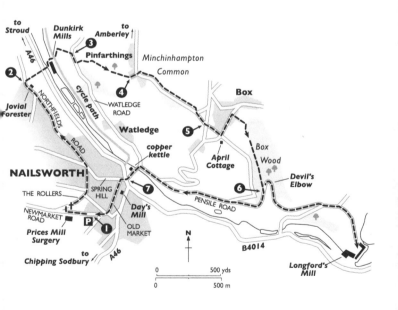

2. Just beyond The Jovial Forester pub car park turn right down a steep path to the mills, carefully crossing the busy A46 road at the bottom. Continue towards the mills and follow the track that sweeps left around the buildings, leading to a tunnel passing beneath the old railway line (now a cycle trail). Go through the tunnel and up the 20 steps before turning sharp left up Dunkirk Pitch to reach Dunkirk House.

3. Turn right along Watledge Road and within 90m (100yd) take the footpath up a driveway on your left marked Pinfarthings. To the right of the entrance to Little Orchard go through a kissing gate and follow the narrow walled path to the top, noting the fine views across the valley as you climb. Cross two stiles and bear right through a small spinney. Cross another stile into a paddock, then go through the horse barrier and over the stone stile into the lane beyond.

4. Turn left and continue to the top of the lane. With Pinfarthings Cottage on your left, take the narrow path straight ahead past a telegraph pole. At the road, cross and climb the stony track up on to Minchinhampton Common, taking the right-hand fork. To the right is a conveniently placed seat where you can rest and enjoy the views. Owned by the National Trust, the common is a rare example of unimproved limestone grasslands with ancient grazing rights, and supports an abundance of wild flowers. From the seat continue right along the path, keeping the common edge to your right. When the path passes Beaudesert School take the road to the right, following the school wall.

5. At the road junction carry on straight across to the attractive village of Box. Where the roads meet April Cottage turn left into the village. On reaching the village green, and before reaching the telephone kiosk, turn right down a waymarked footpath. At the first house on the right, pass through two sets of kissing gates and down a narrow path between the wall and the fence. At the bottom turn right, soon passing a stone stile into Box Wood. Continue through the wood, keeping to the lower left-hand path until you reach the road.

6. Look to your left and you will see where the road makes a sweeping right-hand bend – this is known locally as the Devil's Elbow. (A detour of nearly 0.8km (½ mile) past the Devil's Elbow will take you to Longford's Mill, one of the area's numerous historic textile mills. The once-derelict mill and its associated buildings have recently been restored and now form part of an attractive residential complex bordering on the original millpond.) To continue on your way, turn right and follow Pensile Road back towards Nailsworth. From this road you will see the mushroom-capped chimney of Holocombe Mill in the valley to your left. Turn left over the cattle grid and continue along George Street, looking out for the huge copper kettle hanging from one of the buildings. Originally used to advertise an ironmongers shop, the kettle has been in its present position for over 100 years and holds 364 litres (80 gallons).

7. Cross the A46 into Spring Hill and after a few metres turn left into Old Market. On the left you pass Day's Mill, where the stream still runs under the building and the controls for the water wheel and emptying the millponds can still be found. The two millponds once covered some 2½ acres where the bus station now stands. At the next junction turn right at The Britannia Inn and return to your starting point along Newmarket Road to the car park.

Courtesy of Nailsworth Town Council. For more information see www.nailsworthtown.co.uk

DUNKIRK MILLS

Snuggled in the valley to the north of Nailsworth town, Dunkirk Mills is one of the finest woollen cloth mills in the area. The main stone buildings date from 1795–1855 and still house the three large overshot wheels that once powered the mill. The manufacture of cloth ended here in about 1890, after which various parts of the site were turned over to hosiery knitting and the manufacture of walking sticks and umbrellas. Almost derelict by the 1970s, the buildings have since been restored and converted into residential apartments. However, it is still possible to experience the thrill of watching a giant water wheel powering a piece of historic textile machinery during one of the Dunkirk Mill Centre open days (see www.stroud-textile.org.uk for more information).

Three Cotswold Villages

STANTON, LAVERTON AND BUCKLAND

Set on the edge of the Cotswold escarpment, this 'Made for Walking' waymarked route takes you through three picturesque Cotswold villages, with their traditional honey-coloured stone cottages and historic medieval churches. The walk starts in Stanton, little changed in 300 years, and described by Pevsner as 'architecturally, the most distinguished of the smaller villages in the North Cotswolds'. From here you cross fields, stiles and bridges to reach the delightful hamlet of Laverton, and then continue on your way to Buckland, with its Grade I listed church and what is thought to be the oldest rectory in England. A gentle stroll across further fields brings you back to your starting point and some welcome refreshments at a traditional English pub.

DISTANCE:	5.5km (3½ miles) (circular)
TIME:	Allow 1½–2 hours
LEVEL:	Easy
START/PARKING:	Stanton village car park next to the cricket ground on main road heading north out of village (WR12 7NG); parking also available at The Mount Inn for customers only. OS grid reference SP067343 (OS Explorer sheet OL45)
GETTING THERE:	*By car:* Off the B4632 between Cheltenham and Broadway *By public transport:* Train to Cheltenham, then bus no. 606 towards Broadway, with short walk from main road (not Sundays)
REFRESHMENTS:	The Mount Inn, Stanton High Street
LOCAL ATTRACTIONS:	Snowshill Manor; Gloucestershire and Warwickshire Railway

DIRECTIONS

1. From Stanton village car park turn right along the road and then left, just past the memorial and round towards St Michael's Church. This lovely church has some particularly interesting features, such as the grooves on the back pews which is where the shepherds used to tether their dogs. Walk through the

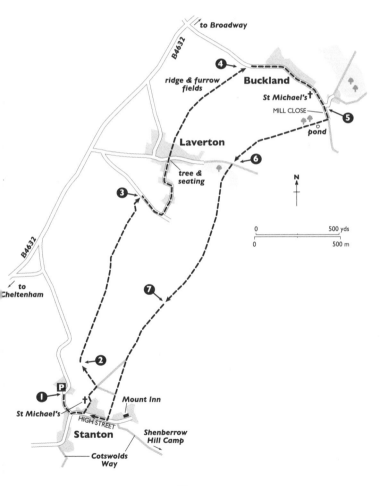

churchyard following the footpath signs and leave through an alley. At the end of the alley, turn left beside the iron railings, pass through a kissing gate over the boardwalk and bear left across the field towards the waymarked sign.

2. Cross the stile and continue following a hedge on your right. Cross another stile and a stone bridge, and continue straight ahead to a third stile and a cross. Still keeping the hedge on your right, cross a stone stile with a wooden top and a bridge. Now continue with the hedge on your left. Cross two further stiles and carry on, with the fence to your right, to a stile and a road that leads into Laverton.

3. Turn right and follow the road through the village around three sharp bends until you reach a tree surrounded by seating. Follow the gravel path opposite for approximately 0.8km (½ mile) into Buckland. Along here you can see the remains of medieval farming in the ridge-and-furrow fields on your left.

4. On reaching Buckland follow the road past the phone box and St Michael's Church. The latter was designer and socialist William Morris's favourite church and he personally paid to have the medieval stained glass releaded. Other interesting features include the medieval scenes of the seven sacraments and some lovely carved beams. The church is well worth a visit if you have time (see special feature, opposite).

5. Where the road bends to the left, take the tarmac drive on your right, called Mill Close. Continue along the track straight ahead and before the gate turn right and go through a kissing gate. Then turn right and follow the fence on your right. The route from here follows a well-used path. Pass a pond on your left and go through two kissing gates, keeping the hedge/trees on your right until you reach a gate. Go through the gate and continue straight ahead across the field to a waymarked pole.

6. Cross over the ancient sunken path and follow the waymark straight ahead towards a marshy and slightly wooded area. Keep going to a stile and a cross, then head towards the left of a large tree. Continuing in the same direction, go through a gate and head for a stile in the far left-hand corner of the field. Cross over, then cross another stile with a bridge in the hedge beyond. Keep following the waymark posts, veering right at the second post towards another post in the distance and a gate in the corner of the field. Shenberrow Hill Camp, an Iron Age hill fort, can be seen above the trees on the skyline from here.

7. Go through the gate and following the path across two more stiles, each with a cross. Then follow the private drive down to the High Street in Stanton. Turn left for refreshments in the pub at the top of the hill, or right to head back to your starting point. Continue down the hill and at the bottom turn right to reach the car park.

Courtesy of Tewkesbury Borough Council (www.tewkesbury.gov.uk).
For similar 'Made for Walking' walks ring 01684 855040.

BUCKLAND CHURCH

For a small church, St Michael's, Buckland, has a remarkably rich array of historic artifacts. Dating largely from the 13th and 14th centuries, its east window contains some particularly beautiful late 15th-century stained glass depicting scenes from daily life. In the north aisle part of an exquisitely embroidered cope (ceremonial ecclesiastical cape) is on display, along with three painted stone panels showing pairs of angels, dating from the 16th century. Also in this aisle is a copy of *Foxe's Book of Martyrs* – a graphically illustrated history of Protestant martyrdom that was widely displayed in churches following the Reformation. In the south aisle look out for the 16th-, possibly 15th-century 'mazer' – a ceremonial goblet made out of maple and topped with a silver rim in 1607. Also of interest are the 15th-century octagonal font and the partly 16th-century pews. Complete your tour by reading the inscription on the tombstone of Thomas Roberts, a 15 year-old boy murdered in 1750 by a local lad from Laverton.

Woodchester Park
Boathouse Trail

*Nestled in a secluded valley not far from Stroud,
this beautiful waymarked route takes you through woods
and pastures abounding with wildlife, past the remains
of landscape gardens, an unfinished Gothic mansion and a ruined
temple, to a string of man-made lakes where dragonflies and
damselflies dance by day and bats feed by night. Bluebells, wild
garlic, lily-of-the-valley and rare orchids are to be found at certain
times of the year, and buzzards, owls and woodpeckers breed in the
woodlands. For those interested in something more otherwordly
than bats and bluebells, the house and grounds are said to
be haunted, with angels, Roman centurions and headless
horsemen taking their turn to scare the unwary.*

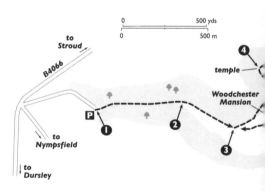

DISTANCE:	5.5km (3½ miles) (circular)
TIME:	Allow 1½–2½ hours
LEVEL:	Moderate, with some steep sections
START/PARKING:	Pay-and-display car park at Woodchester Park (National Trust) off Nympsfield road, 300m (330yd) from B4066 (GL10 3TS). OS grid reference SO797012 (OS Explorer map 168)
GETTING THERE:	*By car:* The nearest motorway junctions are 13 and 14 on the M5 and 18 on the M4; head for the B4066 Stroud to Dursley road, turning off towards Nympsfield as signed posted *By public transport:* Train to Stroud, then bus no. 35 (not Sundays) to Nympsfield, with short walk to park
REFRESHMENTS:	Café at Woodchester Mansion on house open days
LOCAL ATTRACTIONS:	Nympsfield Long Barrow; Uley Tumulus (Hetty Pegler's Tump); Owlpen Manor

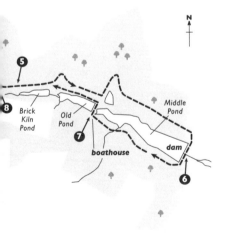

DIRECTIONS

1. From the National Trust car park turn right down the hill, following the orange waymarks of the Boathouse Trail into the woods and heading towards the bottom of the valley.

2. As you emerge from the woods take a look at the pasture to your right, which was restored from a conifer plantation in 1997 in a bid to improve the habitat for the resident greater horseshoe bats. The traditional Welsh black cattle – one of Britain's oldest breeds – that graze the pasture form an important part of the restoration management programme.

3. Bearing left at the waymarked junction you will soon come across the remains of the coach house and stables that once belonged to Woodchester Mansion. Property details prepared for the sale of the estate in 1845 describe these buildings as everything the 'most fastidious Gentleman can desire … coach house for eight carriages … stables with twelve stalls and harness rooms'.

4. Continue onwards to the temple site (now a small ruin). The wooded valley enclosed by the curve of the track contains the remains of terraced gardens that were created in the early 1800s. Historical records give a clue to the gardens' past glory, describing the temple as overlooking Italian-style gardens with fountains playing in ornamental ponds.

5. Enter the pasture where, on sunny days in spring and summer, the wild flowers teem with colourful insects, including scarlet tiger moths and peacock, painted lady and silver-washed fritillary butterflies. Continue downhill from where you will see Brick Kiln Pond, the first of five deep man-made lakes created in the 18th century by damming a small stream and numerous springs. Larch plantations have been cleared from the site so that the historic views across the lakes can be enjoyed once more. Continue to follow the path and fork left at the junction.

6. When you reach the far end of Middle Pond, turn right on to the dam and continue your walk along the south side of the lake. The white water lilies that grow here provide shelter for fish such as carp, roach and tench. The lakes also attract a variety of birds, so watch out for species such as kingfishers and herons, as well as mandarin and tufted ducks, coots and moorhens. In warm weather you will find dragonflies and damselflies skimming the surface of the water.

7. Soon, from a series of boardwalks, the surprisingly ornate boathouse comes into view. Built in the late 18th century and used by residents of the mansion and their guests for outings, it was restored in 1998 when the roof, windows and floor timbers were replaced. Bats use the roof space as a stop-off point on their nightly feeding forays.

8. Continue to follow the orange waymarks, taking the left-hand fork beyond Brick Kiln Pond. After a while you pass Woodchester Mansion on your right, built from the 1850s onwards by William Leigh, a wealthy ship owner from Liverpool, but left unfinished after 16 years' work. Currently in the process of restoration, it is now a Grade I listed building, which can be visited during open days. After the house, climb the path back to the car park.

Courtesy of the National Trust. For more information see
www.nationaltrust.org.uk and www.woodchestermansion.org.uk

BATS AND BADGERS

Woodchester Park is nationally renowned for its bats and badgers. The endangered greater horseshoe bat has breeding roosts in the mansion, where it lives during the summer months, emerging at dusk and dawn to feed on insects. Other bats found here include the common pipistrelle, lesser horseshoe, Daubenton's and long-eared bat. Badgers are equally abundant, with 12 main setts excavated in the sandy soils of the wooded valley – one of the largest concentrations of badger setts in Britain. The badgers are intensively monitored as part of an ongoing research project into the badger behaviour and possible links to bovine TB.

Useful Contacts

**Cotswolds Area of Outstanding
Natural Beauty and Cotswolds
Conservation Board**
Fosse Way
Northleach
Gloucestershire
GL54 3JH
tel: 01451 862000
email: see online contact form
www.cotswoldsaonb.org.uk

Cotswold Canals Trust
tel: 01453 752568
email: mail@cotswoldcanals.com
www.cotswoldcanals.com

Cotswold Way National Trail
tel: 01451 862000
email: cotswoldway@cotswolds
aonb.org.uk.
www.nationaltrail.co.uk

The Countryside Agency
tel: 01242 521381
www.countryside.gov.uk
*(For more details regarding public rights
of way see: Out in the Country – Where
you can go and what you can do)*

Gloucestershire Rights of Way
tel: 01452 425577
email: prow@gloucestershire.gov.uk
www.gloucestershire.gov.uk/prow

**Nailsworth Tourist
Information Centre**
4 The Old George
Fountain Street
Nailsworth
Stroud
Gloucestershire
GL6 0BL
tel: 01453 839222
email: nailsworthtic@btconnect.com
www.nailsworthtown.co.uk

Oxfordshire County Council
Countryside Services
Holton
Oxford
OX33 1QQ
tel: 01865 810226
email: via online contact form
www.oxfordshire.gov.uk/countryside

The South Cotswold Ramblers
A very active group within the
Ramblers organization, providing
a wide variety of led walks for
members and the public as well
as being actively involved in local
footpath matters. Full details at
www.southcotswoldramblers.org.uk

**Tewkesbury Heritage and
Visitor Centre**
100 Church Street
Tewkesbury
Gloucestershire
GL20 5AB
tel: 01684 855040
email: tewkesburytic@tewkesbury
.gov.uk
www.tewkesbury.gov.uk
*(The 'Cotswolds Made for Walking Pack'
@ £5.95 can be ordered by phone on the
above number)*

WILDLIFE

Berkshire, Buckinghamshire and Oxfordshire Wildlife Trust
The Lodge
1 Armstrong Road
Littlemore
Oxford
OX4 4XT
tel: 01865 775476
email: info@bbowt.org.uk
www.bbowt.org.uk

Gloucestershire Wildlife Trust
Conservation Centre
Robinswood Hill Country Park
Reservoir Road
Gloucestershire
GL4 6SX
tel: 01452 38 33 33
email: info@gloucestershire
wildlifetrust.co.uk
www.gloucestershirewildlife
trust.co.uk

RSPB (Royal Society for the Protection of Birds)
www.rspb.org.uk
(As this is a charity, to save time and money, please try to answer queries using the online search facility before emailing via online contact form; if urgent, call 01767 693680 for membership enquiries or 01767 693690 for bird and wildlife advice)

Warwickshire Wildlife Trust
Brandon Marsh Nature Centre
Brandon Lane
Coventry
CV3 3GW
tel: 024 7630 2912
email: enquiries@wkwt.org.uk
www.warwickshire-wildlife-
trust.org.uk

Wiltshire Wildlife Trust
Elm Tree Court
Long Street
Devizes
Wiltshire
SN10 1NJ
tel: 01380 725670
email: via online contact form
www.wiltshirewildlife.org

WWT (Wildfowl and Wetlands Trust)
Slimbridge
Gloucestershire
GL2 7BT
tel: 01453 891900 (press 9 for a list of options)
email: enquiries@wwt.org.uk
www.wwt.org.uk

Heritage Organisations

English Heritage
Regional Office
29 Queen Square
Bristol
BS1 4ND
tel: 01179 750700
email: via online contact form
www.english-heritage.org.uk

The National Trust
PO Box 39
Warrington
WA5 7WD
tel: 0844 800 1895
email: enquiries@nationaltrust.org.uk
www.nationaltrust.org.uk

Natural England
Gloucestershire Office
John Dower House
Crescent Place
Cheltenham
Gloucestershire
GL50 3RA
tel: 0300 060 2484
email: enquiries@natural
england.org.uk
www.naturalengland.org.uk

Travel Advice

By car: go to the AA's Route Planner at
www.theaa.com, under 'Travel and Leisure'.

By bus: go to Traveline at www.traveline.org.uk
(0871 200 2233) or Travel Search at www.carlberry.co.uk

By train: go to National Rail Enquiries at
www.nationalrail.co.uk (08457 48 49 50).

Or refer to *Explore the Cotswolds by Public Transport* and the
accompanying booklets, available at Tourist Information
Centres and from www.cotswoldsaonb.org.uk